W9-AAD-444

PRAISE FOR *MOMAHOLIC*

"I have always dreamed as a woman, wife, and mother for a church that didn't have a shred of self-protection. Help could be easily found in the classrooms marked 'Women Struggling with Depression'; another classroom conversing about 'Gossip' and so on down the long hall: 'Bankruptcy,' 'Loneliness,' 'Unwanted Pregnancies,' and 'Stress.' *Momaholic: Crazy Confessions of a Helicopter Parent* is a wise and hopeful starting place. Hallelujah!"

Amy Grant, award-winning singer/songwriter

"In the constant sleepless haze that I now call my life, I found Dena's story authentic, captivating, and empowering. I don't need another story that makes me feel guilty for not having it all together. I'll never have it all together. Addison will have a better mommy because I have learned this lesson sooner rather than later."

Stephanie Newton, mommy to Addison, age 2

"As a working mom of an eight-year-old and a wife to a sometimes twelve-year-old husband, reading *Momaholic* helped me realize I am not alone in this stressful world of motherhood. We are all crazy at times, but this too shall pass."

Emily Sweeney, mom to Adelle, age 8

"I took a break from completing my daughter's Spanish homework to read *Momaholic* in an effort to understand this poor woman's helicopter condition. Numerous hours later, I realized I had been engrossed in reading about elements of my own life like exhaustion, anger, small miracles and blessings—written by a famous soap opera writer! I was so comforted to know that even famous moms have the same crazy thoughts I have and that our kids can thrive in spite of them. Now back to the homework . . ."

Julie Jayne, mother of Will, age 16,
and Madison and Ryan, twins, age 13

"Being a stay-at-home mom to two girls, ages two and four, and a military wife, sometimes life does seem to be spinning in circles. I enjoyed reading *Momaholic* and realizing none of us 'moms' have it all together . . . even behind closed doors. But having my girls wrap their arms around me and hear them say, 'I love you, Mommy,' makes it all worth it."

Kelly Leasher, mommy to Jerzi, age 4, and Aspynn, age 2

"As a 'helicopter mom' from way back, Dena's book helped me realize that I can still be a good mom even if I give my younger children the space my older children never had. I read *Momaholic* just in time. I have been blessed."

Tammi Storey, mom to Andrew, age 24, Adam, age 23, Samantha, age 12, and Rachael, age 11

"As I constantly search to find the right balance between my family and my job, *Momaholic* helps me realize that my crazy, hectic, sometimes stressful, out-of-control life may not be perfect—but it is perfectly normal. I am reminded to take one day at a time and be the best mom that I can be!"

Dana Bakke, mom to Mack, age 3, and Owen, age 6 months

"As the mom of an eighteen-month-old, reading *Momaholic* helped me envision the mom I might have become. Thanks to Dena's story, my mind-set has changed. I'm determined to do the best I can at being a mom—knowing I can't do it all!"

Mary Rausch, mommy to Ellie, age 18 months

"*Momaholic* is a must-read for mothers of all ages. Dena's story has taught me to take a step back and examine my decisions before acting on them. I feel I will become a better mother because of her story."

Mary Alexander, momma to Holly, age 22, Jamie, age 21, and Katelyn, age 17 (and grandmother to Bana, age 5)

Momaholic

Momaholic

CRAZY CONFESSIONS OF A HELICOPTER PARENT

DENA HIGLEY

THOMAS NELSON
Since 1798

NASHVILLE   DALLAS   MEXICO CITY   RIO DE JANEIRO

© 2012 by Dena Higley

All rights reserved. No portion of this book may be reproduced, stored in
a retrieval system, or transmitted in any form or by any means—electronic,
mechanical, photocopy, recording, scanning, or other—except for brief
quotations in critical reviews or articles, without the prior written permission
of the publisher.

Published in Nashville, Tennessee, by Thomas Nelson. Thomas Nelson is a
registered trademark of Thomas Nelson, Inc.

Thomas Nelson, Inc., titles may be purchased in bulk for educational,
business, fund-raising, or sales promotional use. For information, please e-mail
SpecialMarkets@ThomasNelson.com.

Scripture quotations are taken from the Holy Bible, New International
Version®, NIV®. Copyright © 1973, 1978, 1984, 2011 by Biblica, Inc.™ Used
by permission. All rights reserved worldwide. www.zondervan.com

Library of Congress Cataloging-in-Publication Data
Higley, Dena, 1958-
  Momaholic : confessions of a helicopter parent / Dena Higley.
     p. cm.
  ISBN 978-0-8499-4736-0 (trade paper)
  1. Higley, Dena, 1958- 2. Television writers--United States--Biography. 3.
Motherhood--United States--Biography. I. Title.
  PN1992.4.H54A3 2012
  306.874'3092--dc23
                                                                  2011053191

ISBN-10: 0-8499-4736-0
ISBN-13: 978-0-8499-4736-0

Printed in the United States of America

12 13 14 15 QG 5 4 3 2 1

(I wrote a book about women for women, yet I must dedicate it to a man. Let the irony begin . . .)

To Dan Johnson,

who believed in this project when no one else would.

Who persevered when there was every reason to quit.

Who invested time even when he had none to spare.

Who infected me with his wisdom, energy, and enthusiasm.

You are most certainly the man!

CONTENTS

CONTENTS

PROLOGUE

I can't see. My eyelids are heavy. Can't lift them. Sounds are vague. Blah, blah, blah . . . then words . . . clearer. I still don't have the strength to open my eyes, but it helps being able to hear. Someone is saying, "This way. Put her over here."

My eyes opened. Right in front of my face—and I mean *right* in front—was a jeans-clad man's upside-down butt. Not just any man's butt. I knew that butt, and I purchased those jeans at the Gap. My husband. His familiar voice spoke. He was talking to someone else. I don't know who.

"I think my wife has overdosed or something. Alcohol.

A lot. She fell . . . there's some blood. She passed out. Somebody help me."

Noooooo. He's talking about me. The upside-down jeans backside of my husband was moving up and down, up and down. *Oh wait, no . . . It's my* head *that's going up and down.* There was a very uncomfortable pressure on my abdomen. *Am I being carried upside down over his shoulder? The fireman's carry?*

"Heroic Man Hefts Woman over Shoulder, Whisks Troubled Damsel to Safety." *Didn't I write this scene for Daniel and Chloe last week? Darn. Am I dreaming about my job again? No. This is real.* This was me. The man carrying me was Mark, my husband. He sounded really worried. Why was he worried? It was so hard to think. Fog was swirling inside the various lobes of my brain. *How many lobes does my brain have? Why does my brain even need "lobes"? And what are their names? I can't remember. I can't even remember how I got here. Where is here?*

I was laid down on some sort of bed, and people started poking me with needles, and there was this really bright (and probably unflattering) fluorescent light in my eyes. It hit me. I was in a hospital emergency room. Me. A church-attending Christian woman, mother of four, wife of one man for twenty-three years. Crud-on-a-stick! I knew all about ERs. I brought my husband here when he had his hernia, and my son when he jabbed a bicycle spoke through his leg. I knew how long the wait would be and what this whole hospital thing meant. I was going to be there all night. My mind automatically started clicking: plans . . . schedules . . . agendas. Even in my semiconscious state I went on autopilot: *Adelle has piano tomorrow. Helio has football after school. Connor hasn't finished his history paper yet. Everyone is due to have their teeth cleaned. We need to finalize so many of the wedding plans for Jensen.*

I'm a mom. I simply don't have time to OD.

Part 1

A sweater is something you wear
when your mom is cold.

—ANONYMOUS

1

HOW I GOT THERE

*T*here were a series of events that led up to my spectacular entrance into the hospital. Yes, lots of *events* but only one *reason*. I need to back up a bit to explain.

Are you familiar with the term *flashback*? Of course you are. We see them all the time in movies and books. The television show I have worked on for twenty-five years has perfected the flashback to an art form. So what the heck? Let's flash back . . .

At ten o'clock on that bright Sunday morning, I started sucking on a vodka bottle. *Hmm . . .* that seems a tad early. Not only that, but I continued to suck on it throughout the day. You may ask why. My psychologist sure asked. My mom asked. My kids asked. My husband asked. My nearest and dearest friends asked. It seemed to be a fairly popular question. And it's a very good question. I wasn't homeless. I didn't live in a cardboard box. I didn't rummage through garbage cans, looking for dinner. I was an upper-middle-class, working housewife. I had four kids, one husband, three dogs, and one cat, and in my spare time I was responsible for the entire content of a television show that airs at one o'clock in the afternoon. A show that was suffering dwindling ratings. Ratings that were my responsibility to raise. In other words, I was the head writer for *Days of Our Lives*. It was a stress-filled, nail-biting, soul-sucking job. And it seemed as though I had about a hundred people breathing down my neck all the time.

There were network representatives, producers, various types of executives . . . all of whom were my bosses. I call them the Suits. Some of the men and women did actually include suits in their wardrobes, but execs of both sexes opted for leather jackets and jeans—socks optional—if *casual* was their thing.

I took meetings with the Suits at least once a week, and they were constantly asking me the same question over and over: "What comes next?" "Yeah, Sami shooting EJ in the head sounds good, but then what's next?" "The airplane cabin loses pressure mid-flight and everyone onboard is dead. But then what?" "Hope walks in her sleep, mugs wealthy men, then during the day has amnesia, works as a cop investigating the crimes she has committed . . . *but then what*?"

Soap scribes write thousands of words a day. Seven acts a show, five shows a week. We use ridiculous, over-the-top phrases like *vortex of emotions* and *gut-punched* and *thunderbolt of inspiration*, but we never get to write the words *The End*. And that is why the Suits keep asking the $64,000 question: "And then what?"

That question rang in my ears. I heard it even when no one was saying it. It kept me up at night. It drove me mad. It was tattooed inside my eyelids. Because if you're lucky and blessed, it *never* ends. Soaps were being canceled right and left. We were under a lot of pressure just to stay afloat.

This Sunday happened to occur in May. As anyone who works in television will tell you, May is a very big deal. May is what we call a sweeps month. That means the advertisers of your particular program look very closely at those four weeks and gauge how many people are watching your show. If a lot of people are watching, the network can charge a lot of money for advertising time. But if those numbers dwindle, everyone starts to panic. Especially the Suits.

I'd had a very good May sweeps the year before, but not this year. This year we tanked. We were in the prover-bial toilet. And when that happens, if you happen to be the head writer, the Suits (or Leather Jackets) continually speak at you in harsh, clipped, accusatory, and somewhat frantic tones. Not only that, but NBC was trying to decide if soap operas in general were worth keeping in their daytime lineup. When I first started working in television, NBC had four soaps on the air. Twenty years later, they were down to one. Ours. My bosses kept "reminding" me that the future of *Days of Our Lives* depended on me and me alone. We were an *institution*. We were a *franchise*. We couldn't just fold up our tent and walk away. We'd been on the air forty-five years. If we got canceled it would be for one reason—because I couldn't hack it. They told me this so many times that I actually started to believe them.

I started to feel the weight on my skinny little shoulders. *Days* employed hundreds of people—actors and crew and support staff—many of whom were my friends. If I failed, if I didn't write a compelling story and bring the ratings up, a lot of people—and I mean *a lot* of people—would lose their jobs.

I also had a sentimental reason to keep the boat afloat. MacDonald Carey was a wonderful man, a grandfather figure to millions. He played Tom Horton on *Days* since it first aired in 1968. He died many years ago, but as I wrote the Christmas show every year, I never forgot to have someone hang his Christmas ornament on the tree. It was a symbol. Family never ends. People wanted to be reminded of that. And fan letter after fan letter explained to me in no uncertain terms that the Bradys and the Hortons were the families they'd never had. When Frances Reid passed away recently, it was emotional for me. She, too, had been on the show since the beginning, as Alice Horton, Tom's loving and supportive wife. Frances and the fictional character she played had been a part of my whole adult life. And I wasn't the only one who felt this way. If the show was ripped off the screens of our dwindling-yet-loyal fans, I would feel as if I were orphaning real people. Good people. People who worked hard for a living and just wanted to come home to unwind to their "stories."

But times were changing. And our audience was slowly disappearing. And no one knew what to do about it. The entire landscape of television was morphing. NBC was about to be sold. General Electric had owned the network for years, but the majority of stock was being sold to the cable giant Comcast. No one knew what that meant. Were the new owners going to blaze in and start lopping off heads? Or would they enter uncharted waters tentatively? Would they tread softly or carry a big stick? No one knew. Panic ensued. Blood pressures spiked and nerves were strained and fingers pointed. And most of the fingers were pointing at me. As the takeover grew closer and closer, the wind shifted; it felt as though change was afoot. And not for the better. Especially not for the better if someone new to the scene viewed soaps as an antiquated genre.

But my job wasn't the reason I was in the hospital.

Allow me to continue . . .

My firstborn, Connor, was diagnosed with autism at age four. One month before my hospital trip, Connor completed his sophomore year at Azusa Pacific University with OK grades. But it had been a struggle for him. Countless tutors, pulling all-nighters for a final only to find out he'd studied the wrong material, knowing he wasn't "getting it," longing for friends he didn't have and couldn't seem to make, anxiety, depression. I hated seeing him go through that. I prayed for him. I urged him to keep up the good fight and threw every other motherly cliché I could think of at him. Now he was on summer break. Since the last semester had been such a drain, I felt that he needed a break. So I didn't push him to get a job bagging groceries or washing dishes, although, in hindsight, I probably should have. Instead, he got a part-time job teaching tae kwon do to little kids and learning how to skydive. But his commitments didn't take up much time. Mostly he just self-isolated, and that had me more worried than when he had practically buckled under the weight of a sixteen-unit class schedule.

But he wasn't the reason I was in the hospital either.

My fourteen-year-old baby-but-not-a-baby, Adelle, was becoming a young woman right before my very eyes. Several weeks before my "Chernobyl with the vodka," Adelle had reconstructive surgery on the one foot she has. Some of her toes had been fused together at birth, and they were starting to curl downward. She needed it corrected before her one and only beloved foot became useless. The problem was, once the surgery was completed and her foot was in a cast, she had no mobility at all. She was not supposed to put *any* weight on it. None. We got her a wheelchair, but getting her into the car, the bathroom, or the bed meant we had to carry her. She was understandably irritable and angry. She hadn't wanted the surgery in the first place, and now the most active, independent, and proud teen in the world was forced into a life of complete dependence on others. She hated it.

Even more, her pain was intense and difficult to manage. I slept the first four nights after the surgery on the floor of her room in case she needed meds at three o'clock in the morning.

On top of all of that, there was a ticking clock: she wanted to walk through her eighth grade graduation ceremony just weeks after the operation. Not to mention her sister's wedding, in which she was slated to be the maid of honor. She needed to heal. And time was not on her side.

But all the pain and the stress of her foot surgery didn't push me to the brink. Wait . . . there's more . . .

Helio, my other son, was adopted from Ethiopia at age nine. Several months before my husband flopped me down on an ER table, Helio was enjoying his last semester of eighth grade. During the school year, he had started a sort of entrepreneurial enterprise on campus that was partly shady and partly genius. I didn't know how I felt about it.

The state of California, in all its wisdom, decided to take soda out of school vending machines, thinking that would be a step toward a healthier young generation. But it wasn't against the rules to bring your own soda to school. Apparently a citizen's right to consume caffeinated, carbonated beverages is in the Constitution somewhere. So, while the possession of soda was discouraged, it was not illegal.

Helio saw an opportunity and seized it. He began buying large quantities of canned soda at the store and sold them at school. His mark-up was something like 100 percent. He *would* on occasion take an IOU, but you had to pay 50 percent interest every day until the debt was paid in full. Helio then went online and started studying the stock market. He took the profit he made at school and asked his father to invest in certain stocks for him—stocks he had personally done the research on and had decided to believe in. He did very well, even in tough and volatile economic times. I loved his outside-the-box thinking and his initiative. And I didn't question his motives. He wasn't greedy or materialistic. He loved the game. Still, these kids' parents hadn't necessarily given them permission to drink soda during the school day. Yet they had pockets full of cash. We live in a fairly affluent neighborhood; more often than not, parents give their junior high kids a lot of money, and who knows what they were spending it all on? Something worse than soda? Possibly. So I didn't shut the operation down. Still, I fully expected to be called at any moment into the principal's office and lectured on what a terrible mother I was to let my son do such reprehensible things. It was a conversation I was not looking forward to.

But Helio's antics didn't cause my tailspin either.

Let me introduce my oldest daughter, Jensen. She is so beautiful, so smart, so amazing, so talented. Everyone loves Jensen. But I get to love her the best and the deepest because I am her mother. And she's not just my daughter; she's also my very dear friend. So you can imagine my shock when she came home for spring break her sophomore year at USC and told me she was pregnant.

2

THE LAST STRAW

I panicked. I yelled. I spun out of control. Even the soap opera writer in me cannot come up with words to describe the way I felt. I was angry and heartbroken. My husband, Mark, was devastated. Some young man had impregnated his daughter. His "virginal," beautiful daughter. The one who held such promise. Such a bright future had been thrown away on a night of sex with some guy we barely knew. Why did she do that? We'll never know. She had grown up hearing sermons about abstinence and lectures at school about unprotected sex. It wasn't that she lacked in education. I just didn't understand how this could have possibly happened.

Mark and I unloaded on her. In her defense, she took our rage right in the face. She didn't back down, but she did let the tears flow. She knew her mom and dad pretty well, so I think she had prepared herself for the onslaught.

Mark and I could only yell for so long before we needed to take a breath. Jensen used the pause to finally get a word in edgewise. She fully intended to keep this baby. This pronouncement forced us to stop our tirade and be practical for a moment. Even though we were still numb with shock, we told her we supported her decision completely. Even though Jensen was only two weeks along, we knew instantly we were dealing with a baby here.

Still, things were a disaster on all sides. Mark and I went to bed that night and still were shell-shocked. We turned on each other. Mark felt that this was my fault. I'd babied her. I hadn't explained the facts of life well enough. I sputtered, hoping he was kidding. I was not to blame for this, and he was nuts for thinking so. And on and on it went, well into the daylight hours.

Family dynamics didn't get a whole lot better after Jensen's baby-daddy proposed marriage, Jensen accepted, and I began planning a very expensive wedding.

Mark's gotten perturbed with me many times in our twenty-three years of marriage, and most of the time it has been for a darn good reason. But he had never been *this* mad at me. He told me in no uncertain terms that we were not going to "reward" Jensen's irresponsible sexual behavior with a lavish wedding. I begged him not to think in terms of reward or blame. This was a wedding. That's all. Just a wedding.

I felt that Jensen was giving up enough and facing tough times ahead. No sleep . . . a baby crying all night . . . taking care of a household when she had never cooked so much as a noodle in her life. Being a wife and a mother when she'd never finished being a kid herself. Not to mention varicose veins, a bladder that would never quite work the right way again, breast feeding, leaking nipples that cracked and bled, midnight arguments with her husband about whether the one-year-old should self-soothe or be held. Deciding when to give up pacifiers, when to give up bottles, when to enroll the kid in preschool. She was going to have to make all these decisions when she could have been going to USC football games and sorority parties.

And then there was the long-term plan. Trying to save enough money to buy a house (in this economy)! And even if they could manage to do that, what if she and her husband hated each other by then? They loved each other now, but they didn't know each other. I saw it all in one horrible vision. (You know how in the Bible Saint John had a vision of what heaven was going to be like when Christ returns? It was just like that vision . . . only the opposite.)

Speaking of religion, my future son-in-law was a staunch Catholic, and Jensen was raised super-Protestant. Now, don't get me wrong. I love me some pope. But the

Higley family was very entrenched in our home church. Eventually, this would be an issue. In the sudden onslaught of all these new realities, I was determined to lighten Jensen's load of regrets as much as I could. She'd made a mistake. Had my husband never made a mistake? Had I? Who were we to decide how big her punishment was to be? Regardless of what Mark and I did or didn't do to her, Jensen was going to pay for that mistake more than we could possibly imagine. But I couldn't even go there yet. There was a wedding to plan.

◆ ◆ ◆

I knew my little girl had dreamed and planned for her wedding, as most girls do, her whole life. She was devastated that she would be giving up her college years. I was not going to let her wedding dream be stolen from her too. I didn't work so hard at my job for fancy cars and big houses. No, I wanted to be able to pay for stuff like this. Mark didn't think that was the issue. He said no big wedding. I wasn't going to listen to anything he had to say. The problem is, I'm an emotionally powerful person. So is my husband. We had never issued ultimatums to each other like this before—gone head-to-head—neither of us willing to back down. But that's what was happening. Thus began World War III.

This was so not how I was raised. Marriage is a

partnership. And Mark and I had fallen easily into that groove with our marriage. But when it came to Jensen's wedding, I was calling the shots because I believed with all my heart that Mark was 100 percent wrong. I was frantic with anxiety. Not enough that I was going to change my position, but enough to drive me toward a complete breakdown.

Looking back, it occurs to me that if I'd just "let go and let God," things would have gone much more smoothly. But I didn't. I'm repentant, but I can't go back in a time machine and change what I did. I can ask to be forgiven, but no one can alter the past. So there we were . . . a house divided.

Let's sum up, shall we?

A son struggling with autism, spending the summer locked in his room, taking antidepressants yet still suffering from severe depression. A daughter who had total reconstructive surgery on the only foot she had, so she couldn't walk . . . at all. An unwed daughter who was pregnant, an Ethiopian son who was the head of a semi-sketchy junior high soda cartel, and a husband who hated me. That's on one hand.

On the other hand, an entire television show's very survival depended on me and me alone. What was my response? Prayer? Fasting? Counseling? Nah. Instead, I choose vodka on Sunday morning, starting at ten o'clock and not stopping until, well . . . the hospital visit and the crash and burn of my world.

I OWN IT ALL

The little trip to the ER was all my fault. It was not the fault of the angry husband. Not the fault of my unwed teenage daughter. Not my autistic son's fault. My physically disabled spitfire of a daughter was not to blame, nor was my son who was sure to be expelled the moment his get-rich-quick scheme at school was uncovered. It was also not the fault of the God I believe in and I totally love. It was my fault and mine alone. I couldn't even blame the bad ratings of May sweeps. No, it went a lot deeper than that.

I was angry. I had never been this angry before in my entire life. The sheer power of my anger scared the heck

19

out of me. I didn't know who to direct my anger toward, and that made me even angrier, even more dysfunctional and volatile. Anger consumed me, engulfed me, seeped out my pores and flooded my soul. Sure, my life was going through a rough patch, but there was no cause for this kind of all-consuming fury. I didn't even know why I was so furious. Yet I seethed from head to toe. It's a wonder my hair didn't catch fire from the flames of rage emanating from my brain. During my brief stint in the hospital ER (according to Mark), I shouted at the orderlies, demanding their full and undivided attention. You can imagine how well that went over. I berated the poor ER doctor. I screamed at nurses. I cursed the entire world.

This is uncharacteristic behavior for me. I'm usually too flexible. I bend too far to avoid conflict. It was the way I was raised. The slamming of doors was not allowed. My cool head and calm demeanor were two of the things that first attracted my husband to me. In the workplace, I was famous for being the most facile and serene head writer in the business. As far as my mothering techniques went . . . well, I could dress down one of my kids if the child needed it. But I never hit below the belt (metaphorically speaking) and never hit at all (literally speaking). Once a conflict had been resolved, it never came up again. So this whole "wrath of Dena" thing was a new experience for me.

Back to the ER. After the doctors had purged the remaining liquor out of my body and inserted an IV that spread some sort of lovely cleansing fluid through my system, I was allowed to go home. Mark tucked me into bed, still furious with me but immensely relieved that I was alive; then he stayed up most of the night reassuring Adelle that her world had not collapsed and that somehow, through the grace of God, Mom was going to be all right.

The next day I got up and looked in the mirror. There it was. A broken tooth. I looked like that guy from the movie *The Hangover*. Teeth are a big deal for me. I haven't had much luck in that department. Braces didn't work and, as an adult, I've always had crooked teeth—so breaking my front tooth was just that extra, added bonus for my bad behavior.

The morning after this adventure, I had a regularly scheduled meeting at the studio with my producer (the most wonderful man in the universe) and my co–head writer (equally wonderful). No Suits. Lucky me. I went, humiliated to show them my busted lip and missing tooth, and told them a partial truth: I had fallen in the bathroom and knocked out my tooth. The meeting went on as usual, and when it was over, I went straight to the dentist to get a temporary cap put on. That's when I found out I'd cracked the tooth next to the broken one and it had to be extracted. So one temporary tooth turned into a temporary bridge. The bright side to this was that, while no one completely bought my "I just fell" story, the people I work with seemed unfazed by the fact that I looked like

I'd been in a bar fight. There's a whole pack of crazies at that studio, so this was nothing compared to some of the stuff they'd seen. Apparently there really is no business like show business. No business I know.

That same morning, Adelle slept in because she'd stayed up all night talking to her father about the terrible ordeal her mother had put her through. Helio went to school as usual because he's unflappable. (That doesn't mean he doesn't care; he just goes on about his daily life no matter what. That's what street kids from Addis Ababa do.) I don't know what happened to Connor. He had stayed with his dad at the ER all night keeping a prayerful vigil over his mom, so maybe he slept all day too. Jensen was at the sorority house, enjoying her last months of freedom, which I thought was a good thing since her situation and the ensuing fight I'd had with her dad had set off the whole chain of events. I didn't want her to feel even semiresponsible. Like I said before, they weren't the cause of my crash and burn.

After I got my temporary teeth, the next step was self-examination. And there was only one person in the world capable of untangling the Gordian knot of my temper—my wise friend, psychologist, and pastor, Georgiana Rodiger. She is a genius. Tell her one sentence about yourself and she'll figure out all the rest. She has often told me that she listens to her patients with one ear and to God with the other. She was my only hope. I mean, after all, my way hadn't worked. I was out of ideas.

Of course, when your mentor is that brilliant, you can't just see her right away—there's a long line of screwed-up people in front of you. So I went about my life until I could get to her. The first morning post-hospital was about working and getting teeth fixed and apologizing to my kids. My husband told me some of the insane things I had said—none of which I remembered. And although he was most concerned with the kids' reaction to what had happened, he was also worried-slash-furious with me. I tried to explain to him that the anger that had grown in me became so unmanageable that I had to numb it with alcohol.

"Really?" He said. "With that much? Why?"

"Because I'm angry that you're not being nice about the wedding." *Understatement.*

He didn't want to bring his feelings or actions into the conversation. I was the one who'd ended up in the hospital. He thought our disagreement over the wedding didn't warrant my behavior. I agreed.

"And since that's so not like me, can't you see how desperate I must be?"

He didn't like the word *desperate*. He felt words like *selfish* and *destructive* were more accurate. And he wasn't changing his stance on the whole wedding idea one bit. He brought up the fact that it was also *his* daughter who was pregnant at the age of twenty and in the middle of college and out of wedlock, and that it was also *his* son who was autistic, and it was also true that *his* daughter had just

23

been through surgery, but *he* wasn't sucking on a bottle of vodka at ten o'clock in the morning. As for my "angry" argument, that didn't go over well with him either. He was angry too. I agreed with everything he said.

I had always been the rational one. I had always been the calm one. Why was I unraveling now? Why was anger suddenly my defining characteristic? I told him, honestly, that I didn't know, but I was willing to look into it. Meanwhile, I thought that maybe if some of the day-to-day stress of my life could be removed, that might be helpful. Ruefully, he responded that that would be like putting a Band-Aid on a corpse. He was right.

However, as I went to sleep that night, the one thought that comforted me was, *Perhaps this is a wake-up call for my family. Life's pretty overwhelming for me right now. Maybe they'll see that I need help . . . just with the day-to-day stuff of juggling work and mom stuff. That would be nice.*

The next morning, the alarm clock went off. Mark didn't move. Alarms don't wake him up. I got up. I got the kids up. Once Adelle had dressed and fed herself, I literally and physically picked her up and put her in the car. I lifted her wheelchair to put it in the trunk of the car and almost dropped it, stopping its fall with my thigh. The pain was so intense I thought I was going to pass out. I drove Adelle to school. (Thank God, Helio took the bus.) I lifted my teenage daughter out of the car and into the wheelchair and proceeded to push her into the school building. I got back home. There were dishes to do and a meeting to attend at the studio. No one was awake to assist me in any way. After my meeting at work, I went to pick up Adelle from school. This time I couldn't get the wheelchair to fit in the trunk, so I tried to jam it into the backseat and I banged my broken temporary tooth on the roof of my car. I immediately started sobbing. So much for the wake-up call.

The reason there was no wake-up call, the reason neither Mark nor any of my other kids started hovering around me and worrying about me to the extent that it could have changed my lifestyle, was because I had spent twenty-three (yes, count 'em) years selling them on the idea that I was invincible. I'd convinced them that I was all-powerful.

One night in an ER was enough to tick them off but not enough to change their perception of me. Later, I asked Mark why he didn't get up to help me. He pointed out that he'd gotten very little sleep the night before and that I seemed fine. Except I wasn't fine. I was still angry. I was still a seething mess of a human. But I hid all that in order to maintain my place in the universe. I was a machine. I had to be the perfect mom all the time. I had to make everything right. Like any decent helicopter, I had to hover.

4

THE (VERY BRIEF) ENGAGEMENT

One would think I learned my lesson. But no. I had made a complete fool of myself and hurt my family and injured my body, but that didn't stop me in my tracks and get me to slow down or back off. As soon as my lip healed, I started flapping it again, arguing again with Mark about how best to handle the whole Jensen situation. Jensen's young man, the father of my first grandchild, did the stand-up thing and came to the house to talk to Jensen's father. They sat out on the patio for a long time. Then he left. So I asked Mark what was going on. What had they discussed? Mark was vague, but I understood from him that this very clean-cut, bright, polite young man told him that he had never done drugs and was just about ready to graduate from college. He had a good, steady job waiting for him, and he loved our daughter very much and definitely wanted to be a good father. And someday he wanted to marry Jensen.

When Mark reported the conversation to me later, I didn't know how to feel—except responsible. At that point, I just assumed I was going to end up taking care of the baby. And frankly, I didn't want to take care of another baby. I had four children currently in my care. Enough was enough. I am not one of those women who feel bereft at the thought of my children growing up and leaving the nest. I was ready. I was willing. I was able. I wanted my kids off and flying. When I was their age I couldn't wait to get out of the house and be on my own. No offense to my parents—my childhood was great, and my mom and dad were amazing. But life is for the young! Why the heck not go off and explore?

Mark and I had the money to send our kids to good schools. I was so excited that Connor was going to Azusa Pacific and Jensen was a Trojan at USC. I thought they had one foot out the door. But if Jensen came back home to live—with a baby—this was going the other way. Instead of kids leaving the nest, I was going to be responsible for more? Yikes. Where had it all gone wrong? Little did I know, I had set myself up for this exact situation.

The day after Mark's conversation with Jensen's

boyfriend, Jensen's future mother-in-law called me and said her son came home very confused last night. Apparently, he had specifically asked Mark if he could *immediately* marry our daughter and got no answer. He asked again. Mark seemed to dodge the question again. This was distressing to our future son-in-law. A ring had been purchased, and plans for a romantic proposal had been made. But Mark hadn't green-lighted anything.

It was the first good laugh I'd had in a long time. My husband is extraordinarily ingenious when it comes to cognitive dissonance. It was so like him to misunderstand the entire point of the "May I ask for your daughter's hand?" conversation. Mark must have inwardly inserted the word "someday" into the conversation (twice). I assured all parties involved that this nice young man could, of course, ask Jensen to marry him. If she wanted to, she'd say yes and the yes would be yes. If not . . . well, then Jensen's no would be no. And somehow we'd work out her being a single mother. I told Jensen's potential future mother-in-law that we liked her son very much and that Jensen was a girl who certainly knew her own mind. Hence her current dilemma. So, it was simple. If Jensen said yes, that was good enough for us.

Jensen did say yes. However, I spent every night of the next three months promising her that if she changed her mind at any time, no matter how much nonrefundable money had been spent on flowers and caterers and dresses or how many gifts came in the mail, she could change her mind. No one and nothing was going to *make* her get married. Not her parents, not this baby . . . nothing! She would tear up, thank me, hug me, then promise me that this is what she wanted. (Even though I could tell she was trying to convince herself as much as she was trying to reassure me.)

Meanwhile, Jensen was sick as a dog. She threw up every ten minutes. I clocked one weekend when she managed to only keep down forty milligrams of liquid. I held her hair back and told her it would be all right. But who was I kidding? She didn't have the flu. She was pregnant.

After the proposal and acceptance, reality hit. It was like a scene out of a movie. Mark and I were going to meet, for the first time, our daughter's future in-laws. OK, that's not quite true. We had met them in passing once at a play Jensen performed in at USC, but this was our first chance to really spend time with them. They were lovely people. They were more than happy to invite us to their house all the way across the wide San Fernando Valley in the West Side. They welcomed us with open arms. But, of course, it was awkward. We all were being civilized about the fact that their son had had intercourse with our daughter sometime during spring break and experienced some sort of contraception failure. It was clear both sets of parents were a bit traumatized, but their son was graduating anyway and moving on to adulthood, and they adored Jensen.

So, no harm, no foul. To be perfectly fair, they conceded that the situation was tougher on us, what with Jensen having just turned twenty and having two remaining years of college as well as a promising acting career seemingly thrown out the window. Still, on we went, talking about this and that and making vague wedding plans. Then the talk turned to more practical matters. Where would the newlyweds live and what would they live on while they struggled to get on their feet? It was gently suggested that the bride and groom live with the groom's parents (plenty of space). I suddenly felt as if I were a character in one of my own storylines: gut-punched.

Our car was very silent on the drive home. During the course of three days, we had found out our daughter was pregnant, she would be getting married, and the grandchild we weren't even sure we wanted was going to be taken from us and raised by strangers. Mark's hands gripped the steering wheel so tightly I thought he was going to pull it off its column. It was hard to know how to respond. The offer of free room and board for our daughter (and her husband and child) was so sweet, so practical, so perfect. Of course the newlyweds were going to take a while to get on their feet financially. Not paying rent made perfect sense. But I was freaking out more than ever. The last thing we'd heard before we left was, "You can visit the baby anytime."

5

THE CRASH

It was a downward spiral from there. I went home and said many hurtful things to Jensen, which I wish now I could take back. It was all about me. What had *I* done wrong as a mother? Did *I* deserve to have a daughter who would be so irresponsible? So reckless and thoughtless? In her defense, Jensen took it as well as could be expected. She cried. She was remorseful. But she was solid in her determination to keep this baby and get married. She was grace under fire.

I didn't realize it at the time, but I had selfishly made it all about me and the kind of mother I'd been and all I'd done to deserve better than this. What kind of distorted mind-set had I gotten myself into? Down and down I sank, further and further into depression. I kept thinking: *If Jensen's life was such a disaster after all the love and care I'd poured into it, what was in the future?* My helicopter . . . my hovering . . . my going the extra mile as a mom had gotten me nowhere. I blamed everyone. They were all against me. My husband. My kids. The dogs. Even the cat was in on it, I was sure. I vainly searched back into the past, trying to find where I'd gone wrong.

Despite my incredibly demanding job, raising our kids had always been the true focus of my adult life. Everything I did or said or thought had to do with the kids. I had spent years driving to dance lessons, baseball practices, horseback riding lessons, tae kwon do lessons, football games, wrestling tournaments, tutoring sessions, cheerleading events, play rehearsals, assembly practices, speech therapy, dentist appointments, orthodontist appointments, behavioral therapy sessions. Mark and I even helped build a preschool for autistic kids. If something needed to be done, I did it. If someone left lunch or pom-poms or homework at home, I took it to him or her. I was never late picking anyone up from school or practice or a slumber party. I got up at 6:00 a.m. and started the day with as much positive energy as I could muster. I had a part-time housekeeper, but that didn't mean I had a full-time staff. I still cooked and picked up after and washed clothes even during the odd hours of the night. I took phone calls from my kids in the middle of meetings at work. I took phone calls from work when I was in the middle of feeding my kids. I could pitch a murder mystery story on the phone to a conference room full of people in New York while making pancakes for my family. I once took script notes while standing in line for the Haunted Mansion ride at Disneyland. I was all things to all people.

During most of Connor and Jensen's high school years, I was commuting to New York because I was working for *One Life to Live*. The Suits at ABC wanted as much face time as they could get with their head writer. Understandable. So I showed up as often as I could. But back in California, I never missed a football game or a play or anything of any import to my children at the time. As far as I can count, I only missed one choir concert. I was a workaholic and worse, a helicopter parent. Despite the rigorous demands of my job, I couldn't stop hovering. My record for round-trips from our house to the high school in one day was twelve.

They needed me because everything I did convinced them that they did. They didn't need me, of course, to the extent I had led them to think. And because no human is capable of the strength and support I had promised them with my actions and decisions each and every day of their childhood, there was no endgame but for me to let them down, hurt them . . . betray them.

So, if my life up to this point has been such an unmitigated disaster, why am I writing this book?

Because I don't think I'm alone.

I just got back from a trip to Costco where I perused the book section, giving special attention to the self-help aisle. There are so many women who seem to have all the answers to all my problems. *Steps to a More Healthy You. Stress-Free Motherhood. Control Your Anxiety.*

Apparently, American women are either overly stressed or feel their lives lack meaning. I can't relate to either of these topics. My life has plenty of meaning. And while I'm definitely stressed-out, no one has forced stress on me. This is all my doing. I've made my bed, and now I can't lie still in it. These self-help books are of no help at all.

Frankly, I'm fed up. I don't want some well-coiffed woman, smiling at me from a book jacket, giving me more things to do. I've got plenty to do, thank you. My plate is full. At the same time, I'm not so unhappy that I want to abandon my life in search of a deeper relationship with the universe. What I *want* cannot be summed up in a book or a program or a series of CDs. What I want is to be adored and worshipped by everyone in my family, by everyone at work, and by everyone I ever have met or ever will meet. Of course that's not going to happen. It's unrealistic, self-indulgent, grandiose, and unattainable. More important, it's the last thing I really *need*.

What I need is to figure out how I got into that ER room in the first place, because, as I admitted before, if my life was out of control, I had no one to blame but myself.

It was pure insanity. My insatiable desire to be needed drove me to madness. Why did I need to be needed so much? Why did I enable my kids and allow them to control my schedule, my emotions, my time, and my life, and then turn around and resent them for doing so?

I don't mean to come across like a hypocrite, knocking self-help books while I'm writing one. This is just the story of my journey. Maybe you've been on a similar one.

I know I sound like a big whiny baby. Many parents go through more horrible disasters than my hot mess. No one in my family had died. No one had been kidnapped. No one had cancer. It was simply that my helicopter had crashed.

But this is not a balanced slice of my life. There are so many things about my family and my life in general that I love. I need to lighten up. I gave you the wrong first impression of my husband and kids. I need to focus on the good things. My children are exceptional and amazing, and my husband is my soul mate. I have a great job, a fabulous family, and a blessed life. Yet I almost threw it all away.

May we start over? Meet my family, the greatest people on the face of this earth!

CONNOR

What can I say about my firstborn? Connor was a delight from the beginning. I loved being pregnant. I was twenty-eight years old when I got married and my husband was thirty-two, and there was no time to waste. Our first attempt ended in a miscarriage. We tried again. By then I was thirty. But that pregnancy took. I was healthy. I felt great, and it was an easy birth. And he was beautiful, a perfectly shaped porcelain doll. And he'd look at you with these eyes . . . these wise eyes.

Rolling over, sitting up, walking . . . he hit all the milestones. And his laugh . . . oh my gosh, he had a contagious, hearty laugh. He loved to give hugs and smiled all the time. But no words. Not one. Not *bye-bye*, not *Mama*, not even *Dada*. Nothing. And he didn't really point to things. And he didn't hold his own bottle . . . not once.

I knew something was wrong, but it took a while for me to get anyone else on board with this idea. Twenty-plus years ago a smiling, laughing, hugging baby couldn't mean autism. Not according to my pediatrician or my family or our friends or his speech therapist, or anyone. Until we saw an expert. Until we realized we weren't getting a whole lot of eye contact from our son. Until it was pointed out to us that he wasn't playing with toys in a normal way. He couldn't sit still and listen to a story. He didn't make his toy cars go fast; he just lined them up in an orderly fashion. Autism. By the time the *A*-word entered our lives, we'd had another child. A daughter. Jensen. She came out of my body all pink and squishy, not a porcelain doll at all. And she didn't look at us with wise eyes. She looked bored and hungry and fussy. She did talk and point and sit still and focus. She was not autistic. She was Connor's first, best friend.

I could fill a book with stories about Connor. Unfortunately, this is *my* tale, which should be labeled cautionary at best. A book about Connor would be a book about courage and strength and overcoming. A very inspirational book. But that is not the book you're reading. Still, to understand my story, you need to know what it's like to be Connor's mom.

Connor was almost seven when we decided it was time to take him out of his special preschool and mainstream him. At the time, autism was a relatively obscure problem, not the epidemic it is now. He wasn't nearly ready for "real" school. He still had no appropriate language skills. If you spoke to him, he would repeat the sentence back to you. That's called *echolalia*. So he echoed you if you asked him a question. But he didn't have the ability to process what the question meant and come up with an appropriate response. It just wasn't happening . . . not on even the simplest level. How would a child like that survive in a regular kindergarten? He couldn't possibly socialize. He couldn't possibly learn, could he? Probably not. But our hand was forced. Was he going to go to kindergarten when he was eight? Nine? Ten? Would he ever be really ready? No. He was seven. It was now or never.

We contacted a small Christian Montessori school in our neighborhood. Would they be willing to consider taking Connor? The owners of the school weren't sure. We'd have to do a practice run.

Mark dropped Connor off for his try-out day. Connor didn't really know what was going on, but he could tell the stakes were high. Mark escorted him to the classroom door, gave him a good-luck high five, then left. He turned to see Connor square his shoulders and enter the classroom. Our fairly mute little boy was terrified. But not a protest was made.

Later that afternoon we got the call. OK. They'd take him. I wept and wept and wept. The teacher was a saint. She saw something in Connor . . . the possibility . . . the hope. I will be forever in her debt.

Connor learned to read by sight but still struggled with anything that had to do with language processing. We tried every therapy or treatment under the sun. Slowly he started to open up just a bit to the world around him.

When Connor was about nine, Mark and I enrolled him in a Lindamood-Bell reading comprehension program, which *teaches* reading comprehension. Most kids are not taught reading comprehension in school; they're only tested on how much they can retain. It works for most kids because "normal" students organically pick up the idea of paying attention to the story so they can get the questions right, get a good grade on the comprehension test, get a great grade in the class, get good report cards in general, get into a good college, and make their parents proud.

Patricia Lindamood and Nanci Bell realized there was a small population of kids who weren't learning reading comprehension by osmosis, so they developed a system of teaching students to truly understand what they were reading. It was a godsend to Connor. We signed him up right away and held our collective breaths and waited for progress.

Mark and I were allowed to sit in on one of Connor's sessions. He read a simple sentence: "Sharks come in many sizes and shapes." He read the sentence out loud flawlessly. But when he was asked what it meant, he said he had no idea.

The therapist then proceeded to spend the next hour having Connor look at pictures of sharks and draw them. Some big, some little, some with a lot of teeth, some dark gray, some light gray. Mark and I had trouble staying awake. After an hour of going over this one sentence, the therapist asked, "So . . . what do you think the sentence was about?" Connor looked puzzled. The therapist tried another question: "What have we been talking about?" Connor again looked confused. Undaunted, the therapist suggested that perhaps they had been talking about sharks.

"Sharks?" queried Connor, as if the idea held great interest for him but this was the first he'd heard of it.

Mark and I burst into uncontrollable laughter. An hour! They had talked about sharks for an *hour*! We couldn't stop laughing. Maybe that was the wrong response, but we had lived with autism for a fairly long time, and you have to take your guffaws where you can get them. The therapist had no problem with Connor's attitude or behavior. On the other hand, Mark and I were asked to leave. We were never invited to sit in on a session again.

Flash-forward. Connor is playing right guard on his freshman football team against crosstown rivals San

Marino High. Overall, Connor was not a great football player, but he did well his freshman year because he was a lineman. His position was simple. Block *that* guy. Either move him this way, or that way. If Connor could have played on the line all four years of high school, he would have rocked the game. Unfortunately, as the years went on, the other players got bigger but he didn't. He had to be moved to positions that weren't a great fit for him.

But this day was an amazing day. Despite his team receiving a penalty for delay of game because Connor had to stop to watch an airplane fly overhead, the game was outstanding. My son was a force of nature. He had blocked his man perfectly. He had done just what he was supposed to do, and he knew it. Not only that, but the whole team jelled—hit hard, ran fast, and won by a landslide. Afterward, the coach huddled the players for a postgame pep talk. He asked if any of the guys had anything to say. Connor raised his hand. "We came, we saw, we kicked their ass!"

Connor is always saying funny things, and they're always quotes from movies. They're not his own material. He memorizes lines from movies. But that's OK. His gift is knowing the perfect quote for the perfect occasion.

Connor is a junior at a wonderful Christian college now. He has tutors, and he works harder than anyone I know. In order to get his high school diploma, he had to take biology in the summer. He spent ten hours a day on biology. He didn't really like the subject. It was so difficult for him; it took him dedicating everything at that time to pass the subject. And pass it he did. He always manages to find a way. But it's a difficult way. It's a lonely way. He is so sweet and yet always just slightly out of the loop. Still, he's one of the best people I know.

He lives in two worlds. He's autistic, so he self-isolates. But he's not so autistic that he doesn't feel the pangs of being terribly alone.

His journey is a tough one. In absolute frustration yesterday he told me, "I just don't want to be autistic anymore."

"I know," I said. "I'm sorry. But you are. Don't let it kick your butt."

Then I went in my room, knelt on the floor of my closet, wrapped my arms around my stomach, and rocked back and forth as I have done so many times when my fears for and sadness about Connor overwhelm me. I meant it when I told Connor not to let autism kick his butt. And I don't think it will. But, by God, it's kicked mine.

7

JENSEN

*J*ensen doesn't know she is beautiful. But she is. That is not opinion. It's fact. And it's not just that her face is breathtakingly beautiful . . . the kind of face wars are fought over. There's more there, deeper waters. She has this look in her eyes like she knows some really cool secret about life. The kind of secret almost no beautiful people know. They're all too busy being beautiful. But not my Jense. She expends no energy being beautiful. She gives it very little thought, time, or attention.

Early on, she became her brother's keeper. This is not what I wanted. She and Connor attended the previously mentioned Christian Montessori school from first through sixth grades. The school was so small there was only one class per grade, so they found themselves together quite a lot. I begged the teachers, "Don't ask Jensen, 'Where is Connor's homework?'" Or, "Please don't ask Jensen to remind her brother to do his report tomorrow." But they did. I don't think it's fair to ask a seven-year-old girl to manage a disabled sibling's life, but there you have it. Maybe it made her a better person. Maybe it burdened her too much. Who knows?

Jense was a fairly good student. She could have been brilliant in the classroom, but she lacked interest. She was a cheerleader but never felt she was higher up the food chain because of it. She sang and toured with the school's most prestigious choir. She was busy all the time. She was also, on occasion, a little overly melodramatic. (I wonder where she got that from?)

She found herself on more than one occasion in conflict with older girls—girls who were less pretty, girls who were just plain mean, who made the mistake of trying to bully or embarrass her. One incident involved having dog food thrown on her. On those occasions tears were understandable, but eventually she developed a thick skin. She was a good dancer, and she worked so hard on it I once saw her slip and fall in a pool of her own sweat. Once she did a dance program while she had the flu. She'd dance, run off the stage, throw up into a cup I was holding, then dance back on with a huge smile on her face.

Jensen can also be a bit of a complainer and a non-starter, but she carries these traits with such aplomb that they almost seem adorable.

The most surprising thing about Jensen is how funny she is. Quick with a quip, a one-liner, or an amusing story, she is sharp, witty, and can do spot-on impressions of almost anyone. This shocks most people. Beautiful women, as a rule, are not supposed to be funny. But Jensen is. And she can scrunch her face into the most preposterous contortions. Still, even with eyes puffed out like some blowfish or her mouth contorted beyond recognition, she manages to be beautiful.

She thinks like a writer. I guess that's from growing up listening to her mom and dad talk about story structure and character arcs and such. She shows no interest in writing, but I wouldn't be surprised if her acting talents and her writing abilities someday melded.

Jensen has insight into the human psyche far beyond her years. She can pick up on a character trait or problem a lot sooner than most do. She comes to me at the breakfast table with these most astounding observations about people, and she blows me away.

Her other defining and completely contrasting characteristic is that she is a flake—truly the laziest person I know (sweaty dancing notwithstanding). But because she's wise, she *knows* she's lazy and a flake. And she doesn't care. I've physically pulled Jensen out of the house to get to some of her dance competitions. She was a good cheerleader, but at her school they'd hardly ever practice, mostly just sit around and talk about boys and clothes, so that was a perfect fit for her. She once recently bemoaned the fact that she never played high school sports, that she thought she could have been fairly good at volleyball. I reminded her that people who play sports have to attend practice.

"Oh, right," she said. "Never mind."

She is a brilliant sister. As I said before, she took good care of her older brother, but she also allowed him the honor of returning the favor by letting him take care of her any way he feasibly could—sticking up for her against bullies, teaching her the finer techniques of some of the more difficult video games, stuff like that. They had a good thing going because Jensen *decided* to be a good sister to someone who was locked in his own world. She decided this when she was little more than a baby. And she's never gone back on that decision. That's how kind she is.

She's a good sister to Adelle too. Like any teenage girl, Adelle has her moods. And if there's one thing Jensen understands, it's *moods*. Jensen is an expert at mood swings. I, too, have been known, on occasion, to dip my toe in the pool of moodiness. But Adelle is downright brilliant at feeling emotions she simply refuses to communicate. And when she's . . . (pause, searching for the right word) . . . edgy, everyone in the family gives her space and time and respect. She eventually pulls herself out of it, but it's got to be her choice. Sometimes she shares her burdens with me, sometimes not. But Jensen seems to be the safest person in the family for Adelle to talk to. Once again, that's because Jensen has chosen to build a relationship with her adopted sister. Jensen and Adelle, of course, look nothing alike . . . seeing as Adelle is Asian. But they do share one common trait. They're both beautiful. Maybe Adelle and Jensen bond over being moody, beautiful young women. I don't know. I don't care. I just love that they love each other. They even send each other notes . . . I mean real, written notes . . . not just on Facebook.

They love a good mystery and can unravel any story plot—a necessary tool in order to survive in the Higley household. When they banter at the dinner table, they finish each other's sentences. But they are not just cerebral with each other. They wrestle. (Both are freakishly strong.) Sometimes they just plain irk each other when both are in high dudgeon. Ah, sisterhood.

Jensen is awesome with Helio. Their relationship is the easiest of all. Their love for each other is fun to watch. Of course, because Helio is Jensen's little brother, she teases him mercilessly. And I mean *without mercy*. Not to worry. He can dish it out as well as take it.

It's funny (ha-ha *and* strange) that our kids fall into two camps. It's often Jensen and Helio versus Connor and Adelle. But that kind of division doesn't last long. Jensen is usually the glue that brings us all back together.

Jensen will go toe-to-toe with her parents when she believes she's in the right. That is no small feat. As you might have discerned by now, Mark and I are over-the-top, opinionated, passionate people. And we can almost always corral our boys. But our girls, well, that's a different story altogether.

Jensen's been the object of some of my best parenting moments and some of my worst. She's seen me commit acts of grace and mercy and blessing. She's also seen my self-centered, ugly side. And she loves me anyway.

Isn't "anyway" a wonderful word?

Not all that long ago we had a dinner party at our home. One of my newer friends commented on how caring Jensen is. I was kind of surprised that she'd formed that conclusion about my daughter's personality having such a short exposure to her. My friend pointed out that when Jensen was speaking to her, she really looked her in the eyes, truly cared about what they were discussing. Who can say that about a nineteen-year-old girl? Maybe that's why Jensen's level of interest in their conversation touched her. Lots of young girls want to talk at adults or avoid them altogether, but very few want to listen. Jensen listens and cares.

She has struggled with her relationship with God (wow; as if no one else has) but is in the process of learning how to lean on Him. Especially lately.

That's our Jensen in a nutshell. She vacillates wildly from hardworking, caregiving prayer warrior to mildly disinterested college student to someone who is just down-right bored. From intense loyalty and love to flakiness and laziness—sometimes in the same week, the same day, or even in the blink of an eye.

Sometimes she's wiser than flaky. Sometimes she's more flaky than wise. Her flakiness got the better of her once . . . just once . . . and it changed her life forever.

8

ADELLE

In the jungles of Vietnam near the Cambodian border, a woman gave birth to a baby girl and left her on the doorstep of a small hospital. When she was just hours old, a doctor performed a lifesaving surgery on her. Why those doctors bothered with her, we don't know. We do know she had some sort of intestinal blockage; she has two scars on her lower abdomen proving that the first time the docs went in, they missed. So they went in again. The hospital couldn't have been more than a simple clinic with the most rudimentary equipment. Limited skills, limited supplies, limited time . . . patience . . . money. Here was a little girl whose birth mom was nowhere in sight.

No father. No family at all. No one to pay. But someone saved her life anyway. They randomly called her Tran
Kim Dao, named after one of the doctors or nurses or
orphanage workers, but it was meaningless . . . had nothing to do with her biological family. Mark and I (when
the time came) had no trouble changing it to Adelle, our
Addie-Boo.

Why did her biological mother abandon her? We'll
never know. My guess is that she took one look at the
baby she had just birthed and freaked out. An infant with
one leg and fingers fused together. Did she even know who
the father was? Prostitution is rampant in that part of the
world. Was she all alone? Scared? Horrified? These are
questions only heaven can answer. And by the time she
gets there, I have a feeling Adelle will just be so delighted
to see the woman who gave her life that she won't care
enough to ask. I'd like to think that Adelle's birth mother
walked away from her child praying that somehow, some-
way, someone would care for this child better than she
could. I believe that Adelle's birth mother committed her
child into God's hands. And God said, "Good idea." A
mother's prayer is a powerful thing.

Back in Pasadena, Mark and I were going about our
lives. Connor delighted us by starting to talk . . . sort of.
Jensen was an adorable joy. Yet, I got an itch that I couldn't
scratch. Trolling online one day, I connected up with a
small adoption agency in Port Angeles, Washington. Why

them? I don't know. What was my motivation? Mark and I never once thought about all the poor, starving children in the world and how we should help them. That would have been a wonderful reason to adopt. But I must confess it wasn't ours. I just came to breakfast one morning and announced to Mark: "If I don't adopt a baby, I'll die." Mark just looked at me. We were still fairly young . . . in dog years. We could biologically have another baby. But it felt sort of like, *Been there, done that. It has to be adoption . . . the greatest, most exciting adventure of all.*

My husband is used to this type of hyperbole from me. After all, I'm a soap opera writer. So is he. But he is much more grounded as an artist than I am. He's written other things. I'm just a daytime drama hack. And sometimes I speak like the characters in my TV show. He said yes. I called the agency and told them we were in the market (it sounded like we were buying a house), but we didn't want a perfectly perfect child. We did not want to get into a bidding war with some young infertile couple. We had developed some amazing advocate chops helping Connor try to overcome his autism. We felt capable to take on another challenge.

Yada, yada, yada. Time passed, and one day the phone rang. We heard of a baby in Vietnam with some physical issues. They didn't know if it was a boy or a girl, and they didn't know what was wrong with the baby. (I'd been having dreams of holding a baby with a missing body part.

Seriously.) So I tell the woman on the other end of the line to look into it. We hear nothing. Then, out of the blue, we get a photo of a baby who is about seven months old, prone, on a concrete floor, holding her own bottle with these little mitts that are her hands and with only one leg sticking out from under her tattered dress. I felt the room spin. (Cue the special effects.) That was *my* daughter! My itch was scratched. Now we just had to bring her home.

Did I say "just"?

It was horrible. The hoops we had to jump through were exhausting. It was as if we were trying to smuggle a terrorist into the country. It seemed like the Vietnamese government was against the adoption of a baby they clearly didn't want; the state of California and the INS were hopelessly stonewalling us at every turn. (And this was before 9/11.) I actually remember screaming into the phone at an American government official who was making the process a living nightmare. I then proceeded to rip the phone out of the wall. Mark was not amused. I, on the other hand, thought it would have made a great act 3 tag to *Days of Our Lives*. (I warned you that the line between reality and fantasy blurs for me.)

There are so many stories about Adelle it would fill an entire book to tell them all. For example, my husband advertised to sell his beloved vintage Porsche convertible to pay for the adoption. And the first (and only) call he got for the car was from a Vietnamese man, currently living in

L.A., who had been born in the same province as Adelle. Totally a coincidence. I don't have time to go into all the miracles involving Adelle, but I will share one more story.

We finally got the all clear to go to Vietnam to get baby Adelle. I didn't go with Mark because someone had to take care of our other children and work so we could afford what was turning out to be a very expensive endeavor. Plus, I was afraid if I went, I'd end up adopting everyone. Sometimes I have no self-control. Mark, on the other hand, knows how to identify a specific job and get it done.

When Mark got there, Adelle was very sick. Rubella had ravaged all the children in her orphanage, and she never fully recovered. Weeks before Mark got there, another couple arrived to pick up their baby with their pediatrician in tow. Now, it seems extraordinarily cautious to bring a doctor with you when picking up a baby you've already agreed to adopt. But I thank God every day they did. This physician passed by Adelle's crib on his way to examine another baby, took one look at her, and told the orphanage workers that if she didn't get medicine, she wouldn't make it through the night. Then, without waiting to be asked, he reached in his black bag, pulled out a hypo of antibiotic, and stuck it in her little butt. That one shot was enough. She didn't get well, but she clung to life long enough for Mark to get to her.

If Mark hadn't arrived in Vietnam when he did, Adelle

would have died. But God had other plans. Mark and Adelle bonded over pretzels on the ten-hour drive from the orphanage through the jungle back to Saigon. As he held her in his lap, she reached in his pocket and put his sunglasses on her face. They were in love from that moment on. As soon as they got to Saigon, Mark took Adelle to a clinic and got her some meds. It was ten more days until they got the all clear to leave the country. She was malnourished and frail, but they made it home.

And, not that this has to do with anything, but baby Adelle threw up inside of Mark's shirt pocket when she got onto her first airplane. It was father–daughter bonding at its finest.

When Adelle got home, she was seventeen months old and weighed seventeen pounds. During the day she smiled and laughed and hugged and loved and lived life on the best terms it had to offer. But at night she was covered in head-to-toe welts. They only appeared on her skin at night. I think they were hives of some sort. When they erupted, she did too. She would scream till the wee hours of the morning. I'd stay up with her, walk up and down the halls of our tiny house, and feed her so much iron-fortified formula she actually began to smell like a carburetor. Eventually, the night terrors went away and she settled into life as a Higley and started to gain weight. It wasn't long before she was downright chubby. Of course, all that baby fat went away as she grew into a gorgeous young woman with almond-shaped eyes, golden skin, and shiny, black hair that falls down to her waist. I call it mermaid hair.

Adelle is currently in high school. She's had several hand surgeries to separate her fingers. She has three fingers on each hand and a thumb. Her handwriting is flawless and her artwork is beautiful and her piano playing amazing. She also has had a prosthetic leg since she was two. As she's grown, she's had to have new legs built for her, on the average of one per year. She no sooner gets a new leg than she starts to nick it up, tear it up and bang it up. Her "legs" are visual proof of her nonstop, rough-and-tumble lifestyle. She's a cheerleader and volleyball player. She loves horseback riding. She sings, dances, never walks when she can run, never runs when she can skip. And when she skips, she is happy.

As I sort of hinted at earlier, Adelle has her moods. Because of her first year and a half in the orphanage, and because of being abandoned at birth, there is a place deep down inside her where she doesn't let me in. I call it her "survival cave." What a lifesaving coping mechanism it must have been to help her survive as an unloved, uncared-for baby, alone, in a crib with no mattress, in the wilds of one of the poorest countries in the world. But she is loved and cared for now. Actually spoiled and pampered. And as the years go on and she continues to feel safe and secure, my prayer is that God will light a candle in that cave and let her know that He was always with her, even when she was a tiny baby, and that she doesn't need that cave anymore.

With or without her cave, her strength of character has been hard earned. She's formidable. My suggestion is, don't ever cross her. I'm a very strict parent. I'm an alpha female all the way. I'm one strong cup of coffee. People know not to mess with me. I'll take my kids on and put the very fear of the Old Testament God into their lives. At work, give me a conference room and a story worth fighting for and I can make powerful, grown men take a step back. But when Adelle's in one of her moods . . . she puts me back on my heels.

Once, she had done something simultaneously brilliant and horrible. It involved the Internet. She was in big trouble. I really laid into her. I took away her phone, her iPod, and her computer. Her response was not one of regret or remorse. Instead she looked me right in the eye and asked me, "What are you going to do next? Take away my leg?" I went into my bedroom and sobbed. Mark asked me what had happened. I told him I was happy she'd felt safe and comfortable enough to challenge me in such a way. But man, can she cut the very heart out of you. Her survival instincts are almost otherworldly. She's fabulous and she's fierce. And I love her so much it hurts.

The summer before last, our family did a little project in conjunction with our best friends. Adelle had been writing some poetry and journaling about her disabilities on the Internet. Our friend Jim picked up on them. Being a composer, he wrote a song called, "Love Me for Who I Am." His son, being a film student, directed it. It just won its category at the New York International Film Festival. That's how amazing Adelle is. And she's only fifteen.

She's been back to Vietnam once with her dad. That was a difficult trip for her to make. Even though she doesn't speak about it, she's got to have a certain amount of survivor's guilt. However, I believe that the more time passes and the more she relaxes and lets Jesus love on her, the happier she will become. She can be pretty joyous now. Something happened at school the other day—I can't tell you what, but it involved a B.O.Y.—and you couldn't pry her off the ceiling of my car. I love her when she's like that. I want her to be that bubbly and adorable and overjoyed all the time. But none of us get that, do we?

Of all my kids, I think I'll feel the void the most when Adelle leaves. Despite the music video success, I don't think she'll pursue a life in music. She's certainly talented enough, but her talents cover a pretty wide spectrum of interests, and there's just no telling where her path will lead. Occasionally she talks about going to Africa and taking care of lions. Sometimes she talks about being a psychology major in college. Anything is fine with me. No matter what she ends up doing, look out, world . . . here she comes.

9

HELIO

*H*elio's given name at birth was Subolo, but his birth father, Seife, changed it to Jemberu. He was born in a small village in Ethiopia in November 1994. His birth mother, Katamash, had an adult daughter from a previous marriage, and his father had a second family in another village. (Polygamy is not uncommon in Ethiopia, even today.) Helio's not really sure how many children his father had, but it was a lot. From what I gather, Seife was a truck driver of sorts and not a very nice man. When Helio first came to live with us, he had raised scars on his back from what I can only assume were the results of a series of beatings. I asked, but he never answered or talked about them.

Helio's biological mother died when he was three. He had been very close to his birth mother. She loved him very much. He remembers sitting outside his house, knowing she was sick, waiting for the news. Helio was eventually called into the house. He put his little three-year-old hand on his mother's shoulder, told her good-bye, and she was gone. Helio then went to live with his father's other family.

Seife wasn't around much, and Helio was given into the care of the second wife. She didn't want him, and neither did most of her children. At five years old, Helio's job was to dig holes to be used as latrines. Many nights he would stay out all night or hang out with a friend whose family was very kind to him. He'd play pickup games of soccer in the streets. The winners got to drink water afterward. The losers went without.

The minute Katamash had gotten sick, Seife had gotten worried. It seemed his health was in question too. After Katamash died, Helio's birth father immediately went to the local shaman and sacrificed a chicken, trying to somehow obtain healing. It didn't work. Seife died when Helio was six.

After Seife died, Helio's stepmother sent him to live with his biological mother's oldest daughter, who had just married a policeman and was expecting a child of her own. She didn't want another mouth to feed. She called up a local American orphanage in Addis Ababa, and a man came to pick up Helio and take him away. Terrified, my son trembled as he sat in the car. He waited many miles until the car stopped at a red light. Then he jumped out of the car and ran and ran and ran. He talked his way onto a bus and back to his sister's house. He managed all this when he was barely seven years old.

His sister was furious that he'd returned and drove him to the orphanage herself, demanding that he stay there. The world was his home now, and he had no family.

All Helio had with him to remind him of his beloved birth mother was a necklace in the shape of a cross tied around his neck with a leather band. His first night in the orphanage, the older boys woke him up in the middle of the night, cut the leather off his neck, and stole the cross. Now he truly had nothing.

Halfway around the world, my husband and I became obsessed with the young boys of Africa. We don't know why. With our plates way too full already, we called the sweet woman who had facilitated Adelle's adoption and told her we thought there might be room at our table for one more person. But we were done with babies. And besides, weren't there older boys who needed families? Boys who might be overlooked, lost in the shuffle?

We were sent pictures and videos. When we saw Helio's face—that was it. We were just as certain with him as we had been with Adelle. We just knew he was our son. He had sad eyes and a sweet smile. He spoke no English. Who cared? He was ours, and we had to get him home. Once again, Mark got on a plane and went to get our child. Due to problems at customs in Africa, Mark was the last one out of the airport. There, in the parking lot of the Addis Ababa airport, stood one little unclaimed boy. It was our son holding a sign with the name of the orphanage on it. They saw each other and it was an overwhelming moment. They hugged and cried and hugged some more.

Helio remembers very little about his life in Ethiopia, but he clearly remembers his first days with his new father in the Hilton Hotel in Addis. While they waited for the necessary paperwork to be completed, Helio and Mark embarked on a series of adventures, the most dramatic being Helio's first experience in a swimming pool. Mark had brought a swimsuit for him, and he led his new son by the hand to the edge of the water. Helio's eyes widened. He couldn't communicate with words, but his terrified expression said everything. "What the heck are we going to do in there?" Mark tried to lead him into the water, but the child balked. He pulled back. No way. Mark had to pick him up and carry him into the water. Terrified, Helio clung to Mark and dug his nails deep into his back until blood was drawn. It took many visits to the pool before Helio could relax. Now, when we go to the beach, we cannot get Helio out of the surf. He jumps in the first moment we get there, and we don't see him until the sun goes down. We call him our harbor seal.

Poor Helio had to undergo another name change.

Jemberu just didn't work for us. He had a new life, and we thought it was biblical to give him a new name befitting his new life. We wanted to pick something special, something personal and meaningful. So . . . we named him after a Brazilian race-car driver. I know . . . an Ethiopian boy brought to America named after an Indy racer from South America. It makes no sense. But the name fits.

We brought Helio home, and it was hysterical watching him take a bath. He'd squat in the tub and splash water under his arms as if he were in a river. I gave him a proper bath with a washcloth and soap, and he loved it. I tease him to this day about how much he liked his mommy giving him baths when he was almost nine years old.

Today, sixteen-year-old Helio is a star, a stud, a legend in his own time. Girls flock to him; boys want to be like him. I can't go anywhere with him where someone doesn't know him. He's everyone's friend. He's honest, kind, and so sweet. And as I explained before, he loves the world of finance. I have a feeling he'll be a millionaire when he reaches eighteen. He likes baseball and is a fairly good pitcher, but who knows? He enjoys the camaraderie and competitive atmosphere of sports. One day, when I dropped him off for baseball practice, he was especially nervous because it was his first day with a new team. He must have been about ten years old at the time. He grabbed his bat bag and headed for the field. I jumped out of the car and chased after him, yelling, "Kiss me good-bye, pookie! Come on, my little pookie—kiss me!" Fortunately for him, he's faster than I could ever be, and he got away shouting, "Stay away from me, crazy white woman. I don't know who you are. Leave me alone." We got some attention, and it actually looked like one of the other coaches (who didn't know me) was about to call the cops to have me arrested. Helio saw this and started laughing so hard that I almost caught up to him . . . but not quite.

Now he's almost six feet tall and strong as an ox. Still, he knows he'll always be my little chocolate candy bar. When he's thirty years old, I'm still gonna eat him up. He loves me without question or qualm or judgment. My relationship with Helio is the most peaceful in my life.

MY JOB

I really, really don't want to talk about my job. But a lot of people find it interesting, so I'll give you as quick an overview as possible. I have been the head writer of *Days of Our Lives* for the past three years. Before that, I was the head writer of *One Life to Live*. These shows often get confused with one another because they both have the word *live* in their titles. But they're completely different shows on completely different networks and shot on completely different coasts.

When I tell someone what I do for a living, I get one of four reactions.

Reaction #1: The Apology

"I'm so sorry; I don't watch *soaps*."

My response to this is always the same. "Are you a Nielsen family? Is someone monitoring what you watch on your TV all the time?"

If they say no, then I honestly tell them I don't care if they watch or not. I don't watch them work, so why should they watch me?

Reaction #2: That's So Cool.

"Oh my gosh . . . My mom used to watch that show when I was growing up. We loved watching it in college. Are Bo and Hope still together?" The answer is usually yes. And yes, we are the show that had Marlena. No, we're not the show with Luke and Laura or Susan Lucci.

Reaction #3: Soap Operas Are Evil.

Hmm . . . more on that later.

Reaction #4: I'm Totally and Currently a Fan!

"I saw yesterday's episode. And it was so great. I can't wait for tomorrow." I almost never get this reaction, but it is the only one I really want. Oh well. The reason I never get it is because, sadly, soaps are a dying genre. For the most part, women are not at home folding laundry in the middle of the day the way they were a generation ago. They are at work. And even if they were home, there's cable and the Internet and video games and all sorts of things to entertain them. However, I staunchly maintain that there will always be a need for long-form storytelling. By that, I mean a story that goes on and on and on. Telenovelas are great. But they're in Spanish. And it's difficult to actually gauge how large our audience is since the standard way of measuring it is an ancient and totally inaccurate system developed by the Nielsen company. However, they provide the numbers by which we live or die.

We have millions of people streaming *Days* (for free) on the Internet, and there are a bunch of fans who tape or DVR *Days*. Soaps may move out of the world of network television, and the delivery system of the genre may change, but since the dawn of time, people have needed and will continue to need "their stories."

What I really, really, really, really don't want to talk about is how soaps are written. But this is the question I get asked most often. So here goes: The head writer creates a document of gigantic length. This document covers six months to two years of story for about thirty characters. Each week a team of four to six outline writers break that document down into individual shows in something called a *breakdown* or an *outline*. There is one outline for every episode. We try to do about six a week. These are always in paragraph form. Basically, they are a road map for the show describing scene-by-scene who's in the scene, what they're saying, and what they're doing. Then a team of five to six scriptwriters turns those outlines into shooting scripts. There's all sorts of backstage drama in the middle of the process. The Suits need to have their say.

Sometimes stories are rejected. Sometimes entire weeks are thrown out. Sometimes people storm out of the building. I did that once.

About half a year into my second stint as head writer of *Days of Our Lives*, things got really bad. I had one vision for the show while the executive producer and the network had another. I wanted characters to fall in love, get mad at each other, shoot each other, feel remorse, and then kiss and make up. The network and the EP (executive producer) at the time wanted our characters to sit around for an hour and talk about their *feelings*. At least, that was what I thought they wanted. They were never clear as to what they really wanted. They were just very clear about what they didn't want—namely, the kinds of shows I gave them week after week.

Things got so bad I didn't recognize the show I was watching anymore. What I wrote was not what they were taping and certainly not what was airing. The directors and producers didn't like what was on the page. The actors *really* didn't like what was on the page, so down on the set everything was being changed. What we ended up with was a mishmash. No one's particular vision. No one cohesive story. And so . . . I eventually realized something had to give.

I walked into a meeting with Ken, the owner of the show, and another guy who was the executive producer at the time. Just the two of them. I didn't have my usual stack of scripts or outlines or notes or a briefcase full of papers. I came in carrying two things: my car keys and my cell phone. I didn't even have my purse on me. Strangely, this didn't seem to set off any warning bells with the guys. Instead, I was immediately hit in the face with a thousand notes and changes at once. I was harangued, as I had been week after week, with what was horribly wrong with what I'd written and how it had to be done all over again. I never sat down. The second they took a breath, I calmly held up my hand. I remained standing at the head of the conference table, thanked my bosses for the opportunity to do what so few people are allowed to do. (As I count, only a fistful of people in America did what I did for a living.) Then I picked up my cell phone and my car keys and left. From what I understand, the men in the room began to laugh hysterically. Apparently they believed I was edgy because they thought I was having my period. (I took this as a compliment, having gone through the "change of life" two years prior. Later that day, the executive producer sent me a large bouquet of flowers to *mollify* me while at the same time (according to an accurate source) courting a male head writer away from another show to take my place.

At this point the owner of the show, Ken Corday, someone I had known for twenty-four years, became truly involved. He called me into his office several days later and gave me a pep talk. It went something like this:

"Dena. NBC is going to cancel us unless you give them a dynamite story projection that will knock their socks off and assure them that the fans we still have will stay loyal and that fans who have dropped away will return. Are you capable of doing that for me?"

I said no. And I meant no. Sure, I could write a story that I knew I would love and the audience (or what was left of it) would love. But the Suits would hate it.

"Never mind about anyone else," he exclaimed.

He begged me to go home and write whatever I wanted.

So I did. I wrote and I wrote and I wrote. And what I wrote, I loved. It was total, perfect soap opera in its most pure form. Our lead actress was pregnant in real life. So I wrote a baby switch story with twists and turns and surprises. Ken loved it. The Suits hated it. The network exec told me to my face that the document was a huge disappointment. He then extended his hand for me to shake, thanking me for being someone fairly easy to work with, and expressing regret that things just hadn't worked out. I shook his hand and walked out of the room. Things had sort of played out the way I thought they would.

Long story short . . . I was kept on. This did not make everyone happy. They hated the idea of a baby switch story, felt it had been done to death, and thought *Days* needed a "hip" and "fresh" and "topical" story. But I was old-school, and Ken (remember, he owned the show) was old-school. So he hired a new executive producer who also loved old school, and we went with the baby switch story, and the ratings soared.

King Solomon had gotten it right. There is truly nothing new under the sun.

11

HOVERING

The first time I heard the term *helicopter parent*, I was at a meeting in New York. ABC is always having these meetings about "branding" and "franchising" and staying one step ahead of "the game." And the point of the game is to get the largest possible audience to watch your show. My generation had been classified as a generation of helicopter parents. We hovered. We ran Girl Scout meetings and Boy Scout meetings and PTA meetings. We volunteered to work in the classroom, out of the classroom, around the classroom, in sports, the arts, everywhere. There was no place a kid could escape his or her parent. I'm not saying these things are bad. I'm just telling you what I learned in the seminar.

Then it struck me: I knew some helicopter parents. My son, Helio, eleven years old at the time, invited a friend to the movies on a Saturday morning. The friend said yes, but only after I had conversed with his mother several times. I told her that I would drop the boys off at the nearby movie theater and assured her that I would check what time the movie ended (even though both kids had cell phones) so I would be at the theater the nanosecond the movie ended. I picked the kid up from his house, practically pried him out of his mother's arms, and off we went to the movies.

I bought their tickets. I walked them to their seats. Then I left. But as I was leaving, I ran into the chagrined mother of my son's friend. She had decided that it was far too dangerous for her eleven-year-old son to attend an almost empty 10:00 a.m. movie at our very small, local, suburban movie theater without close supervision. She would sit in the back, where she could keep an eye on her son, but stay she must. She even had her elderly mother in tow. She had gotten her ninety-one-year-old mother out of bed and dragged her to the theater to see a mediocre movie because she couldn't bear the thought of her son "out there" in the world without her.

I found this whole episode both amusing and also sad. Hey, when I was eight, my mom and dad sent me off to walk to the movies two miles away. And . . . I walked six blocks to kindergarten when I was five. Sure, you can argue it was a different time. But, really, was it? Kids my age received sexual advances from teachers, were molested by priests, and observed, on more than one occasion, a flasher. They were kidnapped and beaten. Frankly, it was just as scary a world then as it is now. It's just that back then the TV news was focused on the Vietnam War and Watergate. Let's face it: most kids don't end up with their pictures on the sides of milk cartons, and if they do, it's usually because they're caught in the middle of a tug-of-war divorce. Yes, of course, you have to use common sense and watch over your kids. But to such an extent that they can't individualize and mature and learn basic survival skills? Yikes.

My heart aches when I watch *Dateline* and hear of a story of some poor girl who is taken in broad daylight while walking on her way to school. My brother is a search-and-rescue team member in East County San Diego and I reel when I hear his stories of finding the remains of someone who was just living her life, minding her own business, and then . . . *wham* . . . it is all stolen away from her.

But what do you do with that? This world is what it is. We need to keep our kids smart and safe. But we need to give them *some* space or they'll suffocate. To be perfectly honest, the helicopter parents I know have had kids grow up and do drugs and get DUIs and drop out of college just as often as those whose parents laid back a little. I'm not talking about making your child a latchkey kid; I'm talking about being a smart, reasonable adult trying to raise someone who, someday, we hope, will be a smart, reasonable adult.

There are those parents who take it even a step further and don't just hover; they actively hamper their kid's ability to grow up. A friend of mine was the assistant principal at a high school. He called a student into his office to discipline him about some minor behavior issue. As it just so happened, a new sofa had just been delivered to his office. He had removed the plastic covering seconds before this student entered his office. The kid thought he was being called in because he had drugs in his pocket. He stashed the baggie in the cushions of the new sofa. Imagine his relief when he discovered he'd been called in on a whole other matter entirely and no one knew about the drugs. He left the office and promptly bragged to his buddies that he'd hidden drugs in the administrator's office.

What he didn't realize is, word travels fast, and the administrator soon heard about his boasting. He checked the sofa and, sure enough . . . there was the bag. He called the parents and the student into his office, and you know what the parents did? They threatened to sue the school if they took action against their son.

Anything askew?

When does it stop? Wouldn't it be terribly wrong for a mother who has a son playing NCAA college football to call up her son's coach and demand a meeting to find out why her son isn't playing more? I'm not saying it actually happened; but what if it did? What the heck would be going on there? At his age (eighteen, nineteen, twentyish) it would certainly be up to the player to advocate for himself. If this player was of note, he would have been on a full-ride scholarship, which meant his mommy wouldn't even have the right to question her son's situation since she wouldn't have been writing any checks. Her interference would be embarrassing for her son and humiliating for the coaches. No college program could or should tolerate such behavior. And I'm sure they wouldn't. Not that it has actually ever happened.

When I became a mom, I was determined to do everything right. I was going to be tough but fair. I was going to be strict but fun. I was going to be consistent. And love was going to rule the day. What I fool I was. Not about the love part, but my goal of being perfect. It was impossible . . . and stupid.

My kids are great. Not because I'm a great mom. Or because I sport a bumper sticker on the back of my car touting their fame as STUDENT OF THE MONTH. I'm a self-proclaimed helicopter mom, and I mean that in the worst way possible. My kids are great human beings despite my hovering, not because.

Now, I need to go back to the gruesome details of my helicopter crash. But before I do that, I need to make an even more provocative confession . . .

12

FAITH

As you may have noticed by now, I'm a Jesus person. And I work in TV. This immediately places me in two worlds. On one hand, I go to church and hear from the pulpit about the evils of the entertainment industry in general, TV specifically, and occasionally the preacher will single out soap operas as the ultimate evil in a world of evils. I guess we do write about sex and incest and adultery. But on my show, more often than not, it turns out to not *really* be incest, and the adulterers end up miserable, and good usually triumphs. And all that immoral stuff is in the Bible too . . . so . . .

That was my theological stance. On the other hand,

most of my coworkers scoffed at anything that smacked of religion. The water-cooler rhetoric in TV studios (for the most part) is simple and finite: religion is what's wrong with the world—the cause of all wars . . . the opiate of the masses.

So, without a support system of my own, I guessed it was just me and Jesus. And when I say "just Jesus" that's no small thing. I believe the whole shebang. The Trinity. The fall of man. The need of a perfect redemptive Savior . . . the whole nine yards.

I was raised a Christian, but I walked away for a while. I came back as an adult, not because it was familiar, but because I discovered grace and redemption. And it changed everything for me. So, when it comes to Jesus, I'm all in . . . usually. I love God the Father, God the Son, and God the Holy Spirit. Having said that, I have to admit that, occasionally, God and I have had our disagreements. Now, you might be asking yourself (and rightly so), why, if I believe that God is all-powerful, lives outside of time and space, created all things and knows all things, allows us free will, and loves us unconditionally, I would spin out of control and drink myself almost to death. The answer is simple. Because I'm me.

13

I MUCKED IT UP

This is the most difficult part of the book to write. But it's the reason why I'm writing it in the first place. Maybe it can help. I'm not writing a "how to" book; I'm writing a "how not to" book. And while I generally try not to give advice, I have to admit, I'm worried. I can see the chaos around me. We moms are making these choices and they're killing us . . . literally. And I'm not just talking about my little trip to the hospital. Let's say you're a much stronger, braver woman than I am. You try to be a helicopter, try to hover all the time and raise "the perfect child." The stress is still going to get you. You're still going to have a heart attack or a stroke or something. I actually had a friend who confessed to me that she wouldn't mind a mild heart attack because at least, for a while, someone else would take care of her. How sad are we?

My mom was not like this. Your mom was not like this. So how did all this hovering get started? Not being a sociologist, I can't say. What I can say is that somehow our generation has bought into this whole notion of hovering. Society tells us it's what we need to do. Teachers tell us. Other mothers (both working and non) tell us. There's no escape. We're expected to do everything, be everything, accept absolutely every challenge, take on more and more responsibility and stress until our plates are overflowing. Let me be specific. Here's one example of how the wheels have totally come off the wagon . . .

An acquaintance of mine recently took in two foreign exchange students. It was a wonderful and generous decision on her part. She was going to house and feed them and allow them to attend a private Christian school here in the States. But last time I spoke with her, she teared up and said she just felt like it wasn't working out. She was going to have to move them to another house. She held her head down and "confessed": "I'm a failure."

What? I lovingly got in her face and told her in no uncertain terms that she was never to think that about herself. She tried something and it didn't work. It wasn't a good fit. Not everything in life fits. And the whole point

I MUCKED IT UP

of wisdom is to recognize those moments and correct them. What got her thinking like that? I don't know her that well, but I'm guessing something in her hardwiring made her feel like everything was her responsibility. In life she took none of the credit and all of the blame. I openly confessed to her that I was dealing with the same issues, and I begged her to completely undo her way of thinking about herself and life and take a step back. She told me she wanted to and that her ears were hearing me but that her heart was just balking at everything I was saying. I got it. Heck, I was spending hours in therapy to undo myself. I didn't think for a second that a short chat with me was going to change her life. But at least I spoke truth over her. My heart broke—not just for her but for all the women around me who are so burdened. Women just like me.

I have another friend who was trying to juggle her job as a TV producer and raising two small sons in perfect helicopter fashion. Her life spun out of control as she went back and forth faster and faster until one day, when she just had to be somewhere at an exact time to pick up her son and she was running late. She got in a terrible car accident. She was lucky to walk away alive. She quit her job the next day. She realized she couldn't have it all. Something had to give. Something always has to give.

Well, if the car accidents and the heart attacks don't kill us, something else will. I self-medicated to numb the stress. And I wasn't the first to cope that way. I was watching a

TV show the other night on the history of illegal drugs in this country and how cocaine, during the turn of the century, was considered a cure-all for many ailments. It was the main ingredient in tonics and cough syrups and . . . yep . . . Coca-Cola, which really had cocaine in it at the time. For a nickel you could go to a soda fountain and get a nice cup of Coke and walk out feeling refreshed and peppy. Who were the most frequent customers? Middle-class mothers. Booyah! Maybe this exhausted mommy thing goes back farther than I realized. If I'd been around back then, I would have been the first to belly-up to the counter. At least back then women were tired because they did hard physical labor. Now we have blenders and microwaves and robot floor cleaners. But we're still overly exhausted because we've become more of a personal assistant to our kids than a mom.

I was in the car line the other day to pick up my kids. I was early. I looked around at all the other early moms who had to get there to be first in line; otherwise junior would miss his violin lesson or his tennis lesson or his tutoring session. Those moms were all waiting for 3:05 p.m., when the gates open and teens pour out of the school's campus. Now, to be first in line, you have to get there really early, sometimes half an hour early. What do these women do with their time? Same thing I do. They nap. Yep. Every single woman in every single SUV or minivan around me was sound asleep. And why? Because their lives are exhausting. After they pick up junior and take him to oboe practice or synchronized swimming or trapeze lessons—whatever after-school activity he has—those women (who have been at work all day) have to go home, prepare dinner, clean up after dinner, handle work papers or have sex with their husbands or a thousand other things before they have a chance to sink into the sweet oblivion of sleep.

But sleep often eludes them when they need it most, because the second we put our heads down on our pillows, a thousand different thoughts, ideas, plans, and duties come to mind. We can't relax the way we seemed to in the car line.

We roll around in bed and obsess over the events of the day, playing them over and over in our heads like an endless video. What had we done wrong? Had we done anything right? And what about tomorrow? So many things to do. So many responsibilities. We had to control it all or it would fall apart. Our kids have to achieve perfection in all they do or they'll get left behind, and that would be a catastrophe. We'd be judged the worst mother ever. Or so we think.

I'm not knocking after-school activities. My kids do them and they're important. But you have to keep it all sane and within the limits of what's really doing some good. Yeah, sports teach discipline and self-respect and teamwork. And I think kids need to have something in their lives that they have a passion and a talent for, or they will just sit around the house and watch TV all day. (I can't believe I just knocked television—my bread and butter!) But the way we throw our kids into activities and then sell cookies *for them* and buy them T-shirts with logos and spend thousands on uniforms or costumes . . . not so much. All the "character building" stuff gets shoved aside as the parents sit on booster boards and figure out how to raise money for something that, by now, we've forgotten the point of.

Last week I went to watch Adelle cheer at a football away game in an urban area of Los Angeles very different from our middle-class neighborhood.

Despite our cultural differences, the mothers at the game were doing the same thing the mothers in our neighborhood do. They were selling raffle tickets and hot dogs and giant foam fingers. Why? To make enough money so their kids could play sports.

This is going on at schools all over the country. But where are the not-so-athletic students? I see them at the games. So why aren't they manning the booths and selling stuff? Why are the moms in charge of everything? Our kids study for SATs and AP classes, but how many of them actually know how to make change? And if they really have school pride, shouldn't they "own" the school's fund-raising? Maybe they won't do a perfect job, but that's OK. We insist our children perform perfectly, but that's an impossible demand made more impossible by parents who don't allow their children to fail, learn from failure, and mature into success. And you want to know why we don't step back and let our kids run their own lives? Because we want things done "right" the first time and every time.

I mean, really? I attend football games, and parents work their butts off while kids are goofing around, texting, and, more often than you'd think, getting high under the bleachers. The great conflict of our generation is that we insist our children perform perfectly, but we never give them the chance. Because we want things done "right" the first time and every time.

Helio was recently elected freshman homecoming prince. The student body officers were actually in charge of their own halftime activities. As his parents, Mark and I were ordered to show up and escort him onto the field wearing formal attire. So we did. It was a bit chaotic. The students obviously hadn't thought out every possible detail and scenario. It was, frankly, a bit of a mess. Because they're kids. They've had no experience. They called all the parents out onto the field too soon. They didn't know what to do with us once we got out there. They sort of underthought the whole thing. But by the end of halftime, we knew who had been crowned king and queen of homecoming, and everyone cheered and was happy and it was glorious!

It was glorious because the kids were in charge. Sure,

it would have run a bit more smoothly if they'd left the whole process in the capable hands of parents. But they didn't. And thank God. I wouldn't have cared if the whole thing had been a train wreck, which it most certainly was not. I was just so glad to see adults step back and let the students run things. Those kids owned that halftime show. Now, I say we take that and multiply that times a thousand and you've got a school worth attending.

I am the worst of the worst. I constantly pushed my kids out of the way to do every task myself because I wanted things done the way I wanted them done. That's insanity times ten. I became addicted to control. I didn't even know it until Jensen's wedding made that horrible fact abundantly clear.

14

MY OLDEST DAUGHTER'S WEDDING PLANS

Forget about high school for a minute and go back to my crash and burn.

The wedding plans were moving along. The ceremony was to be held on the grounds of the groom's godparents' auspicious manor. The setting was spectacular, everything Jensen had ever dreamed of. Since she was a little girl, she had imagined herself as a bride *in a garden*, in a lace dress with a beautiful veil and a long train, marrying the man of her dreams. And I was going to be sure that was going to happen.

Also, it had been decided they'd live on their own. The clearest advice Jensen got was from a dear friend of mine who told her, "When you first get married, the two of you should start out in a little rowboat. Just the two of you . . . rowing away. Then you add a baby. And still, you row and row and row. You can visit the yacht—and they can throw down supplies to you from the yacht, but you must not live on a yacht until you can afford a yacht of your own."

And so Mark found the kids a lovely apartment just days before the wedding. Having decided on a home for the bride and groom, it was still chaos everywhere. They'd barely signed the lease when it was time for the wedding. And time was not on our side. Jensen was about to enter her fourth month of pregnancy, and I was not going to have her looking like a Mack truck walking down the aisle. Nor was I going to allow her son to be the ring bearer at the wedding. It was all too Hollywood for me. If she was going to do this, she was going to look svelte and lovely and every inch the perfect bride if it killed me. And it almost did.

While I spent my days obsessed with the wedding, Mark paced the house like a wounded, caged animal. He didn't know what to do or what to think. He often didn't make any sense. His world had crumbled. His daughter was marrying a guy he hardly knew, having a baby while he still totally considered Jensen to be his baby. And his wife wanted to celebrate? To throw a huge party that was going to break the bank? We made good money but not that good. Financially it was going to hurt and hurt a lot. And he had no say. No recourse. His wife had dug in. I was going to do what I was going to do no matter what he said. We'd never been at odds like this before. I took him on toe-to-toe. I loved him so much, and I hated that he hated me for going forward with this wedding. But I just had to do it. We fought like gladiators. We said terrible things to each other, things we can never take back. I hurt him so much during that time. And I paid the price.

THE DAY BEFORE
THE WEDDING

My life was out of control. I was at war with my husband. And I was pretty sure God was on Mark's side about all this.

My whole life I had believed that God insisted I do things the hard way. Stories about my upbringing, including my teen years and my young adulthood, usually end with the phrase, "At least it built character in me."

I had no reason not to believe that God wants us to take the long, twisty, uphill, difficult, painful road. Many times that *is* true, and I assumed it was true this time. I assumed God wanted to build character in Jensen by having her slink off to Vegas for a quickie wedding to punish her. I wasn't having it.

I shook my fist and told God to bring it on, but things were going to be done my way.

As you can imagine, this mind-set made me an absolutely horrible person to be around. Have you ever been around anyone who has decided to override God? Just ask my family if it's any picnic. It's not. And it was a dark and horrible place to live. I hated it. But there I stayed. Why? A big, costly wedding was not what Jensen was asking for. She certainly didn't want to be the cause of her parents' divorce . . . and that's where it looked like this was going. Mark was not backing down, and neither was I. This wedding was going to happen no matter what. God's not on my side? That stinks, but I'm moving forward full speed ahead. All of you (and myself) be damned.

I didn't even consult God in all this. I just assumed He would want this to be more "character building" for both Jensen and me, and frankly, I'd had it with that idea. I'd already experienced all those years of fighting the network, fighting autism, and fighting the difficulties of life in general. God did all this "character" building in me, and now He was going to have to deal with it.

Mark packed a bag, but he didn't leave. Somehow we managed to make it all the way to the ceremony. By that morning I was exhausted—emotionally, spiritually, and physically.

The two days before the wedding, people started arriving from out of town. As soon as I could, I zoomed by the hotel where my sister-in-law was staying. We had some serious shopping to do. Jensen didn't have a going-away dress or shoes for the ceremony. No coat or wrap in case it got cold, no purse, no containment underwear to hide her growing belly . . . nothing. It wasn't her fault; she spent most of her time with her head in a toilet. So my sweet sister-in-law, Jackie, power-shopped with me till we dropped.

Then, the day before the wedding I had planned a fun little bridal spa day at my house. Thank God sister Jackie was there to supervise. I wasn't. I was out running last-minute errands, picking up the wedding dress, having one continuous nervous breakdown—stuff like that.

The rehearsal for the wedding was actually a lot of fun and hosted by the groom's parents. I managed to conceal my inner freak-fest and behaved myself. The dinner after was lovely, with special toasts, the most moving one given by my son Connor—the guy who is usually at a loss for words.

After the rehearsal dinner, Jensen finally got around to assigning table arrangements for the wedding reception. Poor thing. She wanted to be excited, but she felt so sick. And she also realized this was really happening. The college and sorority life she had so looked forward to had vanished. She was marrying a man she hardly knew, and it was for *forever*. She must have taken one look at Mark and me and panicked. We behaved in public, but in private we were ugly. She'd seen us slam doors and scream and throw things. Blame, shame, we did it all in spades. She had a textbook case of a horribly dysfunctional marriage being played out right in front of her. She had to be scared.

Thank God there was one adult who had the strength and the courage to deal with the drama with fortitude. Jensen.

16

THE WEDDING DAY

I got up at six o'clock in the morning and drove to Van Nuys (about twenty minutes away) to pick up a homeopathic remedy my doctor had prescribed for Jensen . . . something that would hopefully give her energy and get rid of the nausea so she could have a wonderful wedding day.

After stuffing the pill into the sleeping bride's mouth, I went to my office to type up the seating chart assignments for the reception. I spent a couple of hours on that and then made the first of what was to be three trips to the wedding site. My first trip was to drop off what seemed like a hundred boxes of votive candles for the reception table. The second trip was to drop off what seemed like a hundred boxes of lemons—because it was summer and the wedding was "nature-themed." Everything involving nature seemed very heavy that morning.

Then I had a meeting with Kenny, the head of the rental company we were using. I gave him some bad news. According to the seating chart Jensen came up with the night before, we needed six more tables for the reception, and the chairs to go with them. He was not a happy camper, but he made a few calls, and the next thing you know, tables, chairs, linens, and dishes arrived for six more tables. Then he said the nicest thing to me. He said I was the calmest, easiest-to-work-with mother of the bride he'd ever met. I thanked him, but as I walked away I had to laugh. My life was on the brink of disaster, but at least I was behaving correctly with *some* people.

I was too swamped with duties to help Jensen get ready. I made a few trips back and forth to the hair salon to drop off and pick up bridesmaids and such. Looking back, I wish I could have been with my little girl more. I see the photos and videos, and the whole getting dressed thing looked like it was fun. But I was outside setting up the ceremony site area along with all the rental guys and my brother and nephews, who had generously donated their talents in sound design. The caterer was wonderful and very much in charge of all that needed to be done on his end. And my friend Karen oversaw everything (a thankless task), and it was all flowing fairly smoothly.

Still, should I have hired a wedding planner? After all, there were more than two hundred people on the guest list, a DJ, a dance floor, expensive wine, a three-course sit-down meal . . . I mean, this was an event worthy of its own TV show. The answer is yes. I absolutely should have hired a coordinator. Should I have made it a smaller event? Of course. As I said before, Jensen never asked for a huge wedding. But I knew she wanted it, so I was going big or going home. Once I'd decided to "go big," I also decided to be the only sheriff in town. But I needed help, which would have meant me giving up some control, and I was neurotic about control. If I controlled the event, then I wouldn't have to deal with my deteriorating marriage, my pregnant daughter, my most deep-seated fears and anxieties, and my spiritual separation from God. Dr. Georgie was there at the wedding and observed my behavior. I thought I was very calm and happy, but she knows the real me. Later she told me it was a lovely wedding but I was borderline psychotic. I don't know what that means. It doesn't sound good. I'm just grateful she included the word *borderline*.

The day of the wedding I did not get a chance to take a shower or wash my hair. I threw some makeup on, tossed myself into my dress, and headed back just as the guests were starting to arrive. I had lost weight and didn't look great. I was sticky and icky. But then, it wasn't my day. It was Jensen's day and she looked . . . well, she looked like something out of a fairy tale.

The day was perfect. The ceremony was emotional. And God was so there. I realized, sitting in that front row, that I had been wrong about God. He was enjoying this day as much as anyone. He didn't care about the money or extravagance of it all. I could feel His joy. He wasn't thrilled with *me* and the way *I* had behaved, but He thought the whole celebration was really first rate.

And so did everyone else. Everyone had a good time . . . most of all, my husband. He walked Jensen down the aisle looking so handsome in his black tux. He looked at Jensen with such love in his eyes. All the angry recriminations and name-calling and rage were forgotten in that moment.

During the reception, Mark really enjoyed himself. He danced with the bride. Then he danced with Adelle, and the two of them made an adorable pair. As it started to get dark, he and his buddies lit up their cigars and walked around, taking in the glory of the evening.

Mark and I only had two problems that night. He didn't ask me to dance. Not once. And I have to admit my feelings were hurt. Secondly, he didn't think I was eating enough. I hadn't been feeling great all day, and I hadn't touched a drop of liquid or a bite of food. Just the thought of eating or drinking anything made me gag. I was dehydrated. At the reception, Mark stuffed a piece of cake in my mouth. Which I promptly threw up.

Bottom line: Jensen got her dream wedding. She was so happy. Her new husband was happy too. Despite my psychotic issues, which I kept to myself, it was just about the nicest wedding anybody's ever been to.

17

FAIRY TALE, FOR SOME

Jensen changed into her going-away-slash-dancing dress about halfway through the reception. It was nighttime and coolish, especially for July in Southern California. People mingled, huddled under the space heaters, occasionally looking up at the beautiful starry sky. Or they partied hard.

The DJ had really gotten the party going, and guests of every generation boogied all night. The dance floor clearly belonged to the priest who had come to bless the ceremony. I don't think there was a dance he missed! My mom and dad danced. Mark's parents danced. Adelle, Helio, and their cousins rocked out. Jensen's new in-laws and their friends had a great time. The bridal party loved the starry evening . . . no one wanted it to end. But it did.

The limo arrived. Rice was thrown. Jensen and her new husband were gone. I couldn't wait to be gone, too. I grabbed her discarded wedding dress, her bouquet, and a few other things, then assured the very generous owners of the house that I'd send the boys for the rest of the stuff tomorrow and demanded my car from the valet, but he had lost my keys. I was paying him an arm and a leg and he lost *my* keys. Finally they were found. As Mark, Helio, and Connor loaded up wedding gifts into the back of our SUV, I took off like a bat out of heck with Adelle and her boyfriend.

Because I hadn't eaten all day, I was in a bad way physically. I had dry-heaved off and on all evening, and new waves of even more serious nausea were coming on. I dropped off Adelle's boyfriend and made it home just in time to vomit up a bunch of nothing into my toilet.

Mark came home to find me shivering under the blankets of my bed. I was shaking from head to toe. I wasn't cold; my body was just in shock. Mark comforted me by snapping great words of wisdom at me, "I told you to eat something tonight. Now look at you. You're a wreck."

"Ya think?"

I put Adelle to bed, told Helio and Connor good night, and went to sleep in Jensen's room. I don't think I even bothered to take off my makeup . . . unheard-of for me.

I slept a few minutes at a time, in stops and starts,

experiencing pieces of dreams. I tossed and turned. I was still shaking violently. The dreams were awful. Faceless people chasing me, attacking me, imprisoning me—me trying to free myself from chains—being trapped in a box or underwater. You get the idea.

Although the sleep was bad, the night didn't seem long. I turned to look at the clock. It was six in the morning. As good a time as any to get up and stop the horrible nightmares. But there was no peace in being awake either.

I sat up in Jensen's bed and looked around at all her things. It had all happened so fast. The pregnancy announcement, the engagement, the planning, the wedding. Jensen hadn't packed anything. The newlyweds were staying at a hotel for two nights in Santa Monica before going back to summer school. Summer school! Married people going to summer school! Two steps away from juice, Goldfish crackers, and a nap. Jensen was a baby. She was a living, breathing cable TV program: *Babies Having Babies.*

Everywhere in her room there were signs of a life interrupted. A receipt for the deposit on her room at the sorority house. Her fall school schedule. A photo of her pledge class. Graded term papers and a syllabus from her medieval art class.

She had asked for a medical leave of one year from school, but now she was going to be a mother. Could she ever find the strength to get back and finish school? It didn't look promising.

What did it all mean now? What had it all been for? I didn't understand. I couldn't think straight. I tried to remember the beauty of the day before. I reached back for a memory but found nothing. I actually drew a blank. I couldn't remember the wedding day at all. But other memories—more distant memories—came flooding into my mind until I thought I would drown in them.

Getting to the hospital with just minutes to spare before Jense was born. Two a.m. feedings that I didn't mind at all. In fact, I loved the quiet hours of just the two of us cuddling.

Just staring at her in awe and wonder and softly singing Beatles songs to my perfect daughter. Propping her up in Connor's high chair way before she was old enough because I simply had to have the whole family at the dinner table. Her first steps while dancing to "China Grove" by the Doobie Brothers.

Four-year-old Jensen laughing and shaking her head as she reenacted the Northridge earthquake, which hadn't been scary at all for her . . . just one big thrill ride.

Watching *Sleeping Beauty* on TV with her and having her little finger point at the screen as she warned Rose, "Don't touch the spindle!"

Dressed as a duck in her first ballerina costume.

Finding a rock in her nose and realizing she'd stuck it in there three days earlier.

Holding her hand while she sat in her little car seat for hours on long trips.

Reenacting the entire story of *The Wizard of Oz* over and over with little plastic dolls. God forbid I should skip a part. She'd correct me, smile, and we'd go on with the story. How happy she was.

Carrying her on my hip everywhere after she rejected the idea of a stroller.

Getting Jell-O with her twice a week in the hospital cafeteria while Connor was upstairs getting occupational therapy.

Helping her with homework. Doing her homework for her. Letting her win at Chutes and Ladders.

Fighting off intense fatigue to drive her to dance class every day.

Writing excuse notes so she could stay home from school when she refused to get out of bed.

Watching her fall asleep on her daddy's tummy.

Trips to New York. Sitting next to her during countless theater excursions.

Watching old black-and-white movies with her.

Laughing at her very bad knock-knock jokes.

Leaving in the middle of a meeting to drive her a few blocks so she wouldn't have to walk in the rain.

Bringing her forgotten homework to school. Bringing her forgotten lunch to school. Bringing her forgotten art project to school. Watching her cheer at football games. Sitting through daylong dance competitions, weeklong competitions. Helping her run through lines for the school play. Retyping monologues so she could read them more easily. Cooking her favorite dinner just the way she liked it. Cooking her favorite breakfast just so she'd eat *something*.

Telling her jerky ex-boyfriends to bugger off. Telling her irrational teachers to bugger off. Telling her hapless school administrators to bugger off.

So many people told me Jensen was my reward for Connor. It was a pretty horrible thing to say. An insult to Connor and to God. But I understood what they meant. Connor was a lot of work. So much therapy and time and money and effort with very little promise of a positive outcome.

But what they didn't understand (and neither did I) was that I was putting all my eggs in one basket. Jensen was the bright promise of the future. Everything was going to go right for her. That's why I did all the driving and late nights and driving and late nights and driving and driving and . . .

Somewhere in the back of my mind I had this idea that I was making deposits in the bank of Jensen's life and that when the time was right, I was going to make a huge withdrawal and the payoff was going to be staggering.

When I was her age, going to college meant everything to me. And when my parents agreed to find a way to make

(below) Connor, age 4,
locked in his own world.

(above) Connor, age 18,
ready to take on the world.

Connor dedicating a big hit to his family in the stands.

Mark and Adelle, day 1 in Saigon.

Adelle, a few months after coming home, recovering from her first round of surgeries.

Adelle, age 13. See what I mean? See that look in her eyes? Fabulous and fierce.

Adelle's first high
school track meet,
100 meters, 3rd place.

(right) Freshman
cheerleader.

(below) Kickin' back in
her everyday leg.

(above) Helio's
orphanage photo.

(right) Picking up
Helio at the Los Angeles
International Airport.

Mark and
Helio getting
to know each
other in Addis
Ababa.

Helio at 16.

In action.

Jensen preparing to be a USC Trojan, age 4, at a pregame football party on campus.

Jensen's engagement portrait.

Mark preparing to give away his little girl. Look how much he loves her!

(Photo by Luke Pickerill)

The Kids.

The Family.

Beaudon Vance Bush. My first grandchild.

it happen, it was a dream come true. Of course, I borrowed tons of money and I needed every scholarship I could get. And I always had a job. But I was living the dream. No one in my family had ever gone to college before.

But something was missing. I was not very pretty, not very rich. And I envied the poise and self-confidence of the girls who had been born to privilege. They were sleek and sophisticated and so sure of themselves. Greek life was out of the question for me. I could barely afford a couple pairs of jeans. Sorority dues and the wardrobe necessary to belong were not going to happen. I really didn't mind. I was being cast in plays and acting my little heart out and loving it. Still . . . I watched the high-rolling donors and their families on the other side of the fence having their pre–football game cocktail parties, and I longed for that life. Maybe I couldn't have it for myself. But someday . . . my daughter . . . she'd have all that and more.

And that's exactly what happened. Jensen's grades were OK, but she just knocked the socks off the audition committee of the theater department. Seven hundred students auditioned for fifty slots in the drama program and she got in.

And because Mark's mom had been a Delta Gamma at USC in the 1940s, Jense was a shoo-in to be a DG also. But she didn't need legacy status to get in. Everyone wanted her. She had all the grace and humor and poised perfection I had always lacked. Best of all, she wasn't forced into this life by me. She wasn't grudgingly living out her mother's dreams for her. She adored her life. She absolutely threw herself into it with abandon and sheer joy.

And then—just like that—it was gone . . . forever.

That morning, the day after the wedding, I sat on her bed in her room and sobbed and sobbed and sobbed. I hadn't cried once from the time she'd told me about the baby through all the wedding planning. There were things to do. And I could only get mad and scream at her so much. She was throwing up all the time and so upset, and I knew that little baby in there was eventually going to pick up on some of this mega drama. Still, I yelled and slammed doors and fought with my husband, but I had never dealt with my real feelings . . . until now. Now it hit me all at once. Without warning, she was gone. I had been promised two more years. I sat on her bed at six o'clock in the morning, looked up at the ceiling, and actually yelled at God, "I was supposed to have two more years with her!" as if we'd had some kind of deal or something.

I knew I was being ridiculous. I behaved as if she'd been killed. She wasn't dead. She was a phone call away. I knew I had no right to such grief. I thought of all the poor parents whose children have been ripped from them by death—cancer, car accidents, murder. Who was I to behave so stupidly?

Having grown up in the church, I'd seen my fellow Christians gather around bereaved people. "Blessed are those who mourn, for they shall be comforted." As horrible as that must be, that scenario had been modeled for me. I knew what that looked like.

But this . . . what was this? This wasn't bereavement in the true sense of the word. This was dysfunction, selfish but super-important broken dreams. I hadn't just cared for Jensen; I had hovered, swam way too much in the soup of her life. Often I had been more of a personal assistant than a mother. And all for what? In many ways this "crash" was more devastating to me than my hospital ordeal. That stupid vodka thing, which happened right after Jensen's pregnancy announcement, had been just a stupid reaction on my part to the shock of it all. But this . . . this was my heart being ripped out of my chest. This time when the helicopter crashed, it was totaled. There was no fixing it. It would never fly again.

18

GROUNDED

I practically ran to Georgie. I needed therapy—and fast! What was wrong with me? I knew there were going to be no easy fixes to my problems, but I had to start somewhere.

Georgie's sweet, eighty-year-old eyes twinkled at me as she sat me down and wisely counseled me. I'm not going to go into the details. Suffice it to say, she used words like "abandonment" and "codependence." At first I couldn't relate to anything she was saying. But little by little, session by session, I started to learn more about myself, more about how I came to be the way I was, and more about the boundaries I needed to build, the choices I needed to make in the future.

But let's face it. Just a few sessions of therapy were not going to fix my multilayered problems. I knew I had a long road ahead of me.

I started monitoring my actions and my feelings. I stuck my nose in my Bible every few hours and started learning cognitive behavioral skills. For the first time in my life, I really asked for help. And I communicated. I talked and prayed and took long walks and tried to breathe again.

It took time, but eventually I found my footing. And whenever I started thinking about Jensen and her husband and started asking myself, *What if they hadn't . . .* I stopped right there. This grandchild of mine was destined to be born. Jensen knew ten days into the pregnancy that she was going to have a baby. Ten days! She could have taken the easy way out. No one would have ever been the wiser. But she didn't. She was committed from the beginning, and I needed to be on board all the way! The fact that she was willing to go the distance with his baby gave me the courage to go the distance, too. But it was a long and difficult journey . . . one I'm still on.

Like a drug addict trying to steer clear of heroin, I've given myself some rules. I did not help Jensen move out of the house. I didn't arrange her furniture in her new apartment. I did not help her open her wedding gifts or bug her about sending thank-you notes or any of the other thousands of things I would have done before.

I'm going to try to behave the same way for all my kids. Connor needs to become a man on his own. He can do it. I have faith in him. I just have to relearn how to be a mom—to stand back and let it happen. That's the tough one because Connor has to learn about everything in life on purpose. He has to *want* to learn about something. He doesn't just pick things up by being around them (except movie lines). When he first went off to college, I had to take him to a grocery store and explain what everything was and what it meant. He didn't know what "produce" and "dairy" were. He knew apples and milk and cookies and meat, but the fact that they were divided into categories? And not the scientific categories he'd learned in biology. No, this was the world of commerce. He was starting with "Dry Cleaning 101" and "Beginning Pharmacy," and on and on it went. The school of life was always in session for him. Can you imagine not figuring anything out by just being around it? Navigating parking garages and doctor's offices? The other day he asked what those big, blue metal boxes on street corners were. His dad answered, "A mailbox." Connor looked confused; isn't that what we have in front of our house? No one had ever explained to him the complexities of mail all the way through. He belongs to a generation who knows all about e-mail, but this whole real mail thing? Where'd that come from?

So we do what we can to pick up the slack, but at the age of twenty-two, he is having to learn some things by doing them wrong. Now that I think about it, he's right up there with Jensen, who is just now learning about paying rent and building a line of credit and all that fun grown-up stuff. Wait till they start paying taxes. *Hee hee hee.*

And my two little ones? Hardly little anymore. High schoolers. I'll love and support them, watch every concert, clock some major bleacher time at all the games. But I won't live their lives for them. They don't need me to do that. They're much stronger than I've ever been. They're already making tons of personal choices. They grocery shop and help cook meals and plan their own wardrobes and make wise choices. Maybe they've stepped up because they're afraid I'll go nuts again. Or maybe because this is the way it was always supposed to be.

We spend more time around the dinner table. Helio will tell us everything that happened to him that day and every thought he's had. No subject is too awkward for him. That keeps things pretty interesting around here. And sometimes very, very gross.

I have more time and energy to just sit on Adelle's bed and let her chat while I listen. And in case you're confused, that is the opposite of hovering. That's mothering. I love to hear about stuff going on at school, mostly social stuff that she only feels comfortable sharing when we're one-on-one. I'm a safer person to talk to now. I don't give much advice unless I'm directly asked for it. I remind her to be kind and honest to others no matter what, and everything will work out OK. Those are two things I'm working on myself. She knows that. I know that she knows that. And now we can be close.

The kids set their own alarms, make their own breakfasts, clean their own rooms, put themselves to bed. I still come in and kiss them at night and remind them I'm on their side. Everyone needs someone on their side.

Mark and I are stepping back in horrified shock and awe, objectively looking from a slight distance at the people we had become in a time of strange crisis. If it had all been just an earthquake (something we Californians are always expecting) or a crash on Wall Street or some horrible disease, we would have probably soldiered on as best we could, with what small faith in God we had firmly tucked away in our hip pocket. Prayer was something we pulled out like an umbrella on a rainy day.

Mark and I will never be the same again. But I love him, and the coolest thing for me is that after all the stuff we've been through he still loves me. What happened to us was simple. I was prepared to sacrifice our relationship to have my own way. I got my own way, but not the way I wanted it. As in all wars, atrocities were committed. Once the dust settled, we both needed to ask for and receive forgiveness from each other. Still fresh in the restoration period of our marriage, we look at each other now with a better understanding of what selfishness can do to a marriage—how it can tear it apart. And we're not about to let that happen.

The most touching part of the wedding was something called a sand ceremony. Jensen and her husband have the amazing blessing that all four sets of grandparents are still living, still married to their first spouses. The pastor at the wedding counted up 304 years of marriage legacy sitting in the front row that day, watching and blessing the nuptials. That's pretty awesome. It was touch-and-go for a while there with Mark and me, but we survived. Remnants of the "time of insanity" still crop up, but we have the proper tools to handle conflict now.

Having said that, we're trying to do a lot of things differently. I'm still trying to learn that our kids are just our kids . . . on loan to us from God, to steer a bit and then let go. I'm in process. Two steps forward and one step back. As I said before, the reason I'm confessing all this to you is because I don't think Mark and I are alone in our struggles. Not that every man is married to as big a whack-job as I am, but there's stuff that goes on. Stuff no one talks about.

How many fathers want to live out their own unfulfilled sports dreams through their sons? How many mothers want to be lauded by their peers as the perfect mother?

And then there's a whole unspoken caste system in place in high school sports, and I didn't know it until I'd had two sons on both ends of the spectrum. His senior year, Connor was lucky if he got to play a few plays in a football game. Sitting in the bleachers, we chatted with the other parents and everyone was pleasant to us and it was what it was. But Helio is very good at baseball, and when we sit in the stands we're looked at and treated a bit differently. Our adopted son is a game-maker, a team leader, and we are accorded the respect that comes with being a part of a talent like his. This does not sit well with me, having been on the other side of the fence . . . where you almost slink into the stadium, feeling lucky to have been allowed to attend at all. And it's no one's fault. These are nice people. No one's treating anyone differently on purpose. It's just that way. Subtle, yet so palpable. And so wrong.

If Connor got to play and things went well, life was good. If Jensen got the lead role, or Adelle sang beautifully onstage, things were great. If Helio pitched a shut-out, it seemed to positively affect the quality of our lives. But they're just kids. And these are just after-school activities. No one's curing AIDS here or solving world poverty. It should just be "good job" and now let's keep going with the real stuff. And if their season is lousy and their grades are disappointing, that does not make life lousy or disappointing.

I experienced exactly what Tim Keller wrote about in his book *The Reason for God*:

If I build my identity on being a good parent, I have no true "self"—I am just a parent, nothing more. If something goes wrong with my children or my parenting, there is no "me" left. . . . If anything threatens your identity you will not just be anxious but paralyzed with fear. If you lose your identity through the failings of someone else you will not just be resentful, but locked into bitterness. If you lose it through your own failings, you will hate or despise yourself as a failure as long as you live. 'Only if your identity is built on God and his love,' says Kierkegaard, 'can you have a self that can venture anything, face anything.'"[1]

That's what I want for my children. Not success in athletics or academics or the arts, but simply to have a sense of self built on a love for their Maker so they can venture anything, face anything. All in all, not a bad dream for any of us to have.

---

1. Timothy Keller, *The Reason for God* (New York: Dutton, 2008), 164–65.

19

GOD IS GOOD—
EVEN ALL THE TIME

When I felt my first grandchild move in my daughter's womb, I was awestruck. He's as much a miracle as his mother was. She's as overjoyed at the anticipation of his birth as I was at hers. What will he be? What will he accomplish? I have no idea. I don't care a whit. I watch my daughter and her new husband closely. It's hard not to start up the old helicopter again and start flying. But I hold off and observe. They know so little about each other; they have been married such a short time. I can just hear it now . . . the script every new couple plays out every night of the week:

NEW HUSBAND: Hi. I'm home.

NEW WIFE: Don't you want to even say hello to the baby?

NEW HUSBAND: I just got home. Can't I even take my shoes off first?

NEW WIFE: I don't think I like your tone, mister.

NEW HUSBAND: Sorry, but I *work* for a living.

NEW WIFE: Oh, and you don't think taking care of our child is work?

Hehehe. I'm sorry to laugh. It won't be funny to them. But it's pretty standard stuff. How they handle it and make it all work is up to them. I'm bowing out of their drama as much as I can. Marriage is going to be tougher to survive than they realize. But they're smart and they're building on a good foundation of mutual respect and love. And if they can weather the stress and the personality changes they're going to experience—good grief, they're so young—then they'll make it.

As for Jensen . . . she's not the same flighty college girl she was six months ago. As her pregnancy progresses, she rubs her ever-expanding tummy and sings to her unborn child. Her life has done a one-eighty, yet she's kept her head on straight and managed to maintain a certain dexterity regarding any humor to be found inside a toilet. Women kept telling her the nausea would subside after the first trimester, but it never did. It hasn't been an easy pregnancy, but she's overcome. Sometimes she's scared. She shares her fears with me. Will she be a good mother? I tell her with utmost certainty that she will be.

I'm fairly certain she will lack the franticness for perfection that I had. The line between her performance as a mother and her own self-worth won't blur the way it did with me. Her life didn't turn out the way I planned. It is in the process of turning out the way it was supposed to. And finally, I am in the process of learning to be at peace with it all.

Looking back, I'm shocked at how alone I felt. It was an isolation of my own making, but I didn't know it at the time. I was convinced I was on my own. My husband had his own opinions. (How dare he!) I wrongly viewed my beloved children as demanding, life-sucking vultures. And I stupidly believed I was expected to fly solo—lifting everyone up with some sort of self-made tether, staying aloft with rusty blades barely able to rotate.

Truth was, I was addicted to being needed. That's what I did best. It had become my identity. I'd lost track of myself. Now I know I need to be me, just a little less me. I don't make the world go round. Never have; never will. I thought if I let down my guard for a moment, it (the entire world) would all fall apart. Of course I didn't talk or act that way on the outside. But deep in my soul, I was sure I could count on no one but myself. And you saw where that kind of thinking left me.

Am I the only woman who's ever felt this way? I don't think so. You may have the gift of encouragement and support, but you're not holding anyone aloft. Not anyone at work, not anyone in your neighborhood, not even your own children. To think otherwise is a dangerous illusion.

Sometimes I imagine I'm in bed after a particularly difficult day. I lie on my back—my arm outstretched, my hand firmly clutching onto something. What? It doesn't matter. Usually something foul, unclean, unholy. Pride. Fear. Uncertainty. Loneliness. And as I lie there sleeping, someone comes and sits next to me. He jostles me awake. I open my eyes. It's Jesus. What does He want? He points to my closed fist.

"Oh no," I say. "That's mine." But He's determined. Finally, I open my hand. My palm is covered in muddy, stinking gook. He takes that foul, unclean mess into His own hand, where it cannot survive, and it vanishes. Still, I want to hold on.

"That's *my* anger, *my* resentment, *my* entitlement, *my* illusions. Let me keep them!"

As usual, He doesn't let me boss Him up. Thank God for God. I was the one who was so sure I was needed. Turns out I was the neediest of all.

◆ ◆ ◆

Helio kicked back in the car the other day when we were driving to pick up his tux for homecoming. He's lived through starvation and loss and pain. Being a high school homecoming prince of a random football game involving no cash prize has been interesting to him and fun but no real big deal. I'll never forget his face the evening we drove from school to get his tux. He just couldn't take his eyes off the sunset. He said, "Mom, look at the sky. Isn't it beautiful? God is reminding us that He is so good."

Amen.

ADDENDUM TO PART 1

Connor came into my office as I was writing the end of this part of the book to tell me he'd neglected to pay the electric bill for his apartment and all of his roommates were in the dark because the lights had been turned off.

I sighed.

"Connor, I asked you about that. I told you that *you* had to take care of signing up for all the utilities before school started."

He swears he doesn't remember that conversation and that I, as his mother, have to do something because they have no lights.

I told him I'm very sorry about that, but he'll have to figure out what to do on his own. He's a grown man now, and at one time or another, we've all had the lights go out. I reassured him with a smile. "I told you about *utilities* before. Don't worry. Just contact the various *utility* departments, and you'll get accounts all current and paid in full, and then you boys will have no more problem with your *utilities*."

Connor stared at me, uncomprehending. "Utilities?"

Then he frowned at me because I was kind of laughing as I remembered his childhood, and I was thinking, *Sharks?*

Don't worry, Connor. All of us miss the main point of things from time to time.

Part 2

My family is like [an] old
sweater—it keeps unraveling,
but then someone figures out how
to sew it up one more time; it has
lumps and then it unravels again,
but you can still wear it;
and it still keeps away the chill.

—ANNE LAMOTT

20

THE BIRTH

F ive Months Later . . .

When you become a grandma, it is no small thing. Well, *he* was small . . . not small for a newborn but too small to have caused all the drama that had previously unfolded in my life. And while his conception had not been welcome news, his birth certainly was.

Jensen was hoping to have her baby on time. But nothing in her pregnancy had gone her way. Why should her labor have been any different? She was one day late . . . then two . . . then a week . . . I didn't know what to make of all this. I had my biological children early. Because I do everything early. I don't like deadlines and try to usurp them whenever possible. Jensen, however, is not as neu-rotic as I am, and she was forced into a holding pattern.

Finally I got the call. She was going to be induced. I packed my bag and rushed to the hospital.

When I had my babies, the last person I expected to have in the room with me was my mom. I love my mom. She's the best mom in the world, but the actual physical act of giving birth didn't feel like anything I wanted to share with her. And vice versa. When I brought my babies home, my mom was Johnny-on-the-spot, taking care of them, burping them, diapering them, and bathing them. But the opportunity to watch me push them out of my body, well, she passed.

I didn't want it to be a big to-do anyway. I had seen the film in my Lamaze class of women giving birth. Not an attractive moment for the mom or the baby. So when I went to deliver my two kids and the nurses asked if I wanted a mirror, I was horrified. Heck to the no.

And a side note . . . Jensen was giving birth to her baby in the exact hospital where she had been born. Only a few changes had taken place since then. For one thing, having a baby is now a group project. Back in the day, it was just Mark and me. But Jensen wanted everyone there. Me, Mark, her brothers, her sister, her in-laws . . . bring them all in! Once that epidural hit, she was the hostess with the mostess.

But when it came time to get down and dirty, she just

wanted *me*. I was honored. I was flattered. And I was more than up to the task. But I worried that my presence in the room might cross the line. I'd set up some pretty specific boundaries when it came to my mommy-ing. I was determined to be Momaholic-No-More. But this offer was too good to pass up. So we agreed to a compromise. As the moment got closer and closer, Jensen would kick everyone out. I would stick around for the pushing and the fun, sweaty stuff . . . until the last moment. Then I would *vámanos*. And at that magical moment of birth . . . it would just be the new mommy, daddy, baby, and the necessary medical team. That way the special moment would just be about the birth of a new family.

So, around eleven o'clock at night, in went the Pitocin. The nurses assured the extended family that nothing was going to happen for the rest of the night, so everyone else went home to bed but me. I slept on a couch in the waiting room.

It wasn't more than a couple of hours before my son-in-law came to get me. It turned out that Jensen was extremely sensitive to Pitocin, and it was game on. I held Jensen's hand as she got down to the nitty-gritty of expanding her vagina wide enough to push seven pounds of person through it.

Soon she was ready to deliver. The doctor positioned herself behind home plate with her catcher's mitt at the ready. The nurses were standing by with towels and various medical whatnots. This was my cue to exit stage right. I kissed my daughter . . . who was still *my* baby . . . and told her I loved her and turned to leave the room. Then I thought of something, a question I simply had to ask her in that exact moment. It was something so important it couldn't wait. So I turned back to ask her and saw a sight I wish I could erase from my memory: the sight of my grandson crowning. I had a perfect angle and a clear shot of my daughter's very private parts looking probably very much the way mine had looked when I gave birth to Jensen . . . a vision I had worked so hard to avoid twenty years ago. There it was—the miracle of birth—in all its icky splendor. And what was the question that was so important that I just had to ask it at the precise moment my daughter was squirting a baby out from between her legs? I can't recall.

And so we welcomed the newest member of the family. His first name is Beaudon. I think it's a made-up name. Who does that—names their kid a made-up name? My daughter, of course. She's not the child of a soap opera writer for nothing. And his middle name is my dad's first name, Vance. Tears flowed.

My mom was in North Carolina to help usher in the birth of my brother's newest child. Yes, I have a grandson and a nephew born two days apart—a very *Days of Our Lives* kind of thing.

So my mom couldn't be there, but my dad showed up

first thing that morning and got to meet his namesake. Both families gathered. A gaggle of grandparents, great-grandparents, aunts, uncles, and friends descended on the hospital. This child who started out as a small cluster of unwanted yet quickly multiplying cells has become the most cherished, adored, loved person ever born. Go figure.

BTW . . .

I wouldn't feel this chapter about the birth of a baby would be complete without my rule about writing "birthing" scenes on *Days*. I never allow my writers to have the characters say, "The baby is perfect! Ten fingers and ten toes."

I hear that all the time. I hate it. Connor had ten fingers and ten toes, and that wasn't any sort of assurance that he wouldn't have trouble in the future. Jensen had ten fingers and ten toes, and that didn't mean she wouldn't break my heart in the future.

Adelle wasn't born with ten fingers and ten toes, and that doesn't mean she's not "perfect." Because she is. So may I entreat you . . . stop this madness! No more counting fingers and toes on birthdays. It doesn't assure you of anything. Just rejoice in the miracle of life—whatever the packaging.

21

A BABY IN CRISIS

Courage is fear that has said its prayers.

— DOROTHY BERNARD

*T*hree months later . . .

I'm honored. I've never been to the NBC offices. But there I was, having been summoned to talk story with the two people who represent the network's voice in our *Days of Our Lives* story meetings. It's a supercool office, and I have a hard time concentrating because all I want to do is look out the window at the three huge escalators at Universal Studios that connect the upper lot with the lower lot.

I'm fascinated because I worked as a tour guide at

Universal almost thirty years ago when there were no cool escalators. We guided our guests down a winding road in bright-pink trams. (Now they're a more appropriate blue.)

My network boss has a view of all this from his office, and it's so difficult for me not to mentally wander back in time to my salad days at Universal when I was in my early twenties and got my first taste of what it was like to be in "show business," albeit not a true taste. I loved being a tour guide, and I met my husband during the second summer I guided. I was very good at my job, giving all the pertinent facts and telling all the right stories. My husband stank. He made stuff up, fell asleep at the microphone, made no effort to entertain . . . until the very end. Then he did this big, dramatic closing and always got a huge round of applause from his guests. I, on the other hand, got nada . . . zilch . . . nothing. But he is a charmer, and I did marry him, so I wasn't too resentful.

I forced my attention away from the breathtaking sight from the Suit's window and forced myself to pay attention to a meeting that was not going at all badly. I agreed with everything that was said or suggested, and I was quite optimistic, despite a new lull in the ratings. Just then I heard my phone vibrate in my purse. My blood went cold. I knew what this message was about and I instantly panicked. *The baby. There's something terribly wrong with the baby.*

However, I was too cool to let my fear show on my

face. We went on languidly talking about this and that, but my casual demeanor was barely masking my inward freak-out festival.

It was critical that the two people sitting in front of me not know what was going on with my grandchild. I remember clearly the time I received Connor's diagnosis. My head writer had become a very dear friend of mine, so I felt safe in sharing my private angst with her. Her response was to fire me, saying, if I had an autistic child, I obviously couldn't focus on the task at hand . . . mainly to be a good staff writer for *Days of Our Lives*.

Twenty years later, I'd learned not to talk much about my role as a mother or wife or even grandmother to my bosses for fear it would be used against me. It's not that these two people weren't personal friends. They were. They'd even been to Jensen's wedding, and I'd given them both cigars the day after my grandson was born. They would have wanted to truncate the meeting quickly, wishing the baby all the best and promising to pray for him, but it was my policy to try to compartmentalize my life as much as possible so no one could say I wasn't doing a good job because I was too busy being a (for lack of a better word) . . . woman. So on and on we sat . . . another hour at least, before we wound up the meeting and parted.

My casual demeanor vanished the minute I hit the elevator. I waved good-bye to the very polite and official assistant who had escorted me through the maze of hall-ways and watched the elevator doors close. Then my face turned ashen. (I know because the inside of the elevator was glass, and I could see my ghostly reflection.) I pushed the G button a million times. It seemed like years before the doors opened. I ran to the parking garage. I couldn't get a signal on my phone. I screeched out of the studio parking lot and headed for the freeway. Finally I had enough bars on my phone to make a call. Mark told me they'd just admitted our grandson to the hospital. I told him I'd be there as soon as I could. I hung up and switched to hands-free as I methodically called person after person to let them know what was going on and what I needed for an overnight stay at the hospital. I shifted into crisis mode and did what needed to be done.

I careened into the hospital parking lot, jumped out of my car, and began to run. I screeched to a halt as I rounded the corner into the hospital room just in time to hear the doctor tell Jensen and my husband what was going on. My grandson, Beau, was in the hospital bed, three months old and looking like a skeleton. The surgeon was appalled that his condition had gone undiagnosed for so long. He was born with something called pyloric stenosis, basically a blockage between the bottom of his stomach and the top of his upper intestine. He had been projectile vomiting for months, and I had grown increasingly worried, but he was getting what I thought was the best of care, and the pediatrician just thought he was having a problem with Jensen's breast milk or some sort of acid reflux situation. Still the baby continued to vomit and lose weight. The day of my meeting with the Suits, Jensen was slated to see the doctors, who panicked enough at the sight of his dramatic weight loss to do an MRI, which found the blockage.

The operation was simple and routine. In fact, the condition appears most frequently in white, male firstborns, which Beau is. What being a male or white or firstborn has to do with how your stomach is formed is beyond me. Most often the problem is discovered when the baby is a newborn, but poor Beau had suffered for months for no reason. Finally, we had real answers and a real solution and real hope for a healthy future for Beau. I'm just glad they knew what was wrong and could fix it, but the worry had taken a terrible toll on Jensen and her husband . . . on all of us. That's the scary part of the story.

Here's the cool part. As much as I wanted to step in and take control, I held back and watched in awe as Jensen rightfully assumed the role of mother. There was no need for me. I mean, she loved having me there, and I could watch over Beau while she got some much-needed shut-eye in the middle of the night, but she was asking all the right questions. She was calling the shots. She was a mom-warrior. She was girded for the fight—pushing down her own feelings and fears and rightly remaining strong and confident for her baby.

Her husband and her in-laws arrived at the hospital around the same time I did. We were all ready to circle the wagons and form a support team, but, frankly, Jensen and her husband had it covered. Their son had been basically starving to death for months and not one doctor had told them what was wrong. Beau was truly skin and bones. My husband, always looking for a way to lighten the mood, dubbed him Megamind, because when a person loses weight, his skull stays the same size. It was sad but true . . . and kind of funny (if we had the strength to go there)—he was this little baby with a giant head. I thought all he needed were electrodes wired to his bald skull and we could plug them into a computer and he could rule the world. No, I'm not on drugs. It's just the way I think to get me through difficult times. And almost losing my precious Beau . . . nothing was more difficult than that.

In this world of instant gratification, I find I'm shocked when I can't just snap my fingers and get what I want. I was used to the fast pace of TV, but medicine isn't that way. We had identified the problem, but now had to wait. The baby had a tube stuck down his nose, all the way to his stomach, pulling out what bile might be left in there so that the surgeon would have a clean shot at unblocking things. It would be twenty-four hours of waiting before the surgery could be performed. We were assured that Beau would be "fit as a fiddle" right after the surgery.

But the look on the doctor's face after the operation

made us realize instantly that Beau was neither fit nor a fiddle. The doctor had never seen blockage like that. The incision she made was twice as long as she'd anticipated. She really had to open him up. She warned us that the recovery was going to be much more complicated than originally planned. It would be a long time before Beau could have any liquid, and then it would be just a couple cc of glucose water at a time until he was ready for breast milk. Jensen put her head in her hands. I thought she was going to lose it. She was so exhausted and scared, and this was *not* the deal she had been promised. I was prepared to do my momaholic thing and take over, when suddenly Jensen raised her head up and said, "Then let's do it."

22

I WANT WHAT
I DON'T WANT

Resentment. Man, that's a tough one. I'm not going to give you the *Webster's Dictionary* definition of the word; I'm going to give you mine.

resentment *n*. a feeling I have when I've done nothing wrong but have been left holding the bag

I started feeling resentful once the panic about Beau began to subside. Jensen was playing a small part on *Days*, and I found myself sharing babysitting duties with Jensen's mother-in-law. I always said I was happy to do it

151

because what kind of shrew doesn't want to take care of her own grandchild? Ahem . . . apparently, me.

I remember how four-year-old Jensen would literally tremble with excitement when my mom came to visit. She'd rush down the stairs of our house and fly into her waiting grandma's arms. That's the kind of grandma I wanted to be. But things were not looking promising.

When I had Beau with me, I was more often than not holding him on my lap while trying to tap out e-mails or documents on the keyboard of my computer, which gave me horrifying déjà vu. That's the kind of multitasking I had to do when I raised my kids. And if that's what a working mom has to do—well, OK. But a working grandma? Yikes.

I watched my mom jump into the grandma role with both feet. She was free—free to focus on each grandchild one at a time without worrying about what to cook for dinner, scrubbing a toilet, doing a load of wash, or splitting her focus between two or three or (gasp!) *more* kids. She assured me that the genius of being a grandma is that you give your entire heart and soul and attention to the baby. You can be calm and present and don't have your focus thrown in a million different directions. And that's why kids love grandmas so much.

Dang. Beau wasn't getting any more of my time or attention than my kids got. I still had the same job, still had other kids to care for, still had my many plates spinning in the air.

When Adelle was little, she solved this problem by setting up a little desk and a toy computer next to me. She'd sit next to me and type away just as her mommy did. Later, she made up her own soap opera, brilliantly titled *Beyond the Sky*. I couldn't always follow all the plot lines, but then a few of the *Days* fans sometimes couldn't follow mine, so I guess (talent-wise) Adelle and I have always been on a level playing field.

Right before Mark brought Helio home from Africa, I found myself between jobs, so I was able to spend plenty of time getting to know my new son.

Having said that, most of my mommying has utilized maybe 60 percent of my brain and 50 percent of my energy. Here I was again, helping to raise generation number two, trying to make bottles, feed a baby, take a phone call, write a document, and hide a baby's cries from a producer on the phone!

That's when my resentment was born. This was supposed to be *my* time. My babies were in high school. As far as being a chauffeur, I could see the light at the end of the tunnel. I couldn't wait for my youngest to start driving. I was *this close* to having my freedom. Then I got saddled with a grandkid.

Let me assure you, I never, ever, *ever* put it in those

terms out loud. I loved the baby. I was glad the baby was in my life. But he was mucking up my plans. And if you know anything about me by now, you know how much I love having my agenda pushed aside.

At this point in my life I'd already written the first part of this book, and I was totally aware of my faults and flaws. Nevertheless, I began to run around like crazy trying to work, take care of my family, and "mother" my grandson—because my utopian idea of grandparenting was not coming true, so I built on the foundation of my resentment and started trying, once again, to be all things to all people.

Mind you, I knew better, but old habits die hard. An epiphany doesn't always lead to a complete lifestyle change. I wasn't hovering as much with my kids, but I didn't apply the same rules to my grandkid. I was determined to be the perfect grandma, and I was wonderful with the baby. I could soothe him and sing all my favorite songs to him, and he was always very comfortable with me. But I was not comfortable with the situation. Just when I'd gotten my "mom" stuff together, I was tricked. I knew that Jensen's husband was working hard to provide and was hardly ever home. I knew Jensen needed some time and space for herself. Been there, done that. So I pitched in and did the best I could, but it wasn't with the best of attitudes. In fact, though no one could see it, I had a very bad attitude indeed.

Then, as things do with me, the situation spiraled out

of control. I don't want to get into details, but I found myself face-to-face again with my own crap . . . the real truth about my resentment, my codependence issues (if you're into the psych rhetoric, which I give you permission not to be), my fear of abandonment, all of it. There I was again, rolling around in the muck and mire of my most dysfunctional characteristics. I was rock bottom . . . again. I smote my forehead. Same song, second verse. Only this time I recognized it. I had to stop. I had to rearrange my thinking, but quick. There was no way I was going to foist all my inner garbage on this baby. He didn't deserve that, and neither did his mom.

I didn't see the baby for a while. I took drastic measures to get my priorities and my entire life in order. To explain how I did that would take another entire book. Let's just say I found help in the form of a group of like-minded, emotionally challenged people. We met regularly and started processing our lives. Through them, more therapy with Dr. Georgie, and input from two other amazingly wise counselors, I worked hard to put my act back together, re-carve out some balance and peace in my life.

When I felt strong enough, I got a chance to be with the baby. I was so excited. I wanted to see my grandson again. As luck would have it, everyone was busy, so for a while, it was just me and the baby.

I held Beau, and it was as if I were holding him for the first time. No personal agenda on my part. No playing the role of weary caretaker. No resentment for taking care of a child I had no part in conceiving. No . . . I just enjoyed being with him all day and into the night. We played and laughed and loved each other. And that love was so freeing . . . so perfect . . . I finally understood what my mom had been talking about all these years. I had been trying to be this baby's second mother because I was worried that his first mom wasn't enough—despite her trial-by-fire in the hospital. I felt my jaw unclench as the truth of life washed over me. This little person had a perfectly wonderful mom and a terrific dad. He was part of a little family of three that was doing just fine without me. And I had the honor and the blessing of being his grandma. Just grandma. And when I allowed that fact to pierce my heart, I suddenly had this incredible desire to be with this child as much as I could. Because I *wanted* to. Not because I *had* to. I wanted to take him swimming and to the zoo and the park and read to him and push him in a stroller and be everything to him that my beloved grandma had been to me. She had been the perfect grandma. And I knew I could be that for Beau, too, because it had been modeled for me. That's why the role of freaky-grandma didn't fit. That wasn't what I knew. But *perfect* grandma. Ahh. I knew what that was. Why hadn't I seen this before? Grandmas are just *love* 24/7. I could do that in a heartbeat.

When it was close to his bedtime, I held Beau's cheek against mine, and he sighed his little baby sigh—and for a moment, the world stopped spinning, the continents stopped shifting, and the world stopped revolving around the sun. Time stood completely and utterly still. It was just Beau and me—in the center of our own vast and glorious universe. We breathed in unison, in and out, in and out. Usually, he's a squirmy little dickens, but he sensed my calm, and he relaxed into my embrace. We stayed frozen like that for an entire lifetime. Then, ever so slowly, I began rocking him and softly singing my grandma's favorite hymn . . .

"Oh, what peace we often forfeit. Oh, what needless pain we bear. All because we do not carry everything to God in prayer."

Then I pulled him away so I could get a good look at him. We made eye contact. I smiled at him, and he smiled back. Then I whispered to him: "Beau, ya know what? It's just like Rick and Louis at the end of *Casablanca*: 'I think this is the beginning of a beautiful friendship.'" And I knew then and there that we'd be bonded for life and that we were going to have many great adventures together. We sat, rocking, contemplating the future for a very long time, while still feeling very present and very content.

And then I gave him back to his mother.

23

HAROLD HAD AIDS

cried for three days after I read *Marley & Me*. That book touched a deep, emotional chord in me. The story of the yellow lab was completely parallel to the story of our first dog. When Mark and I got married, our first child was a furry, giant-pawed Siberian husky puppy named Chelsea. For a while it was just the three of us. Just like the book. Then I had a miscarriage, and, just like in the book, my big, beautiful, blue-eyed pooch loved on me so hard it helped me recover and gave me the strength to try again.

And there was Chelsea, waiting for us at the front door when we brought Connor home from the hospital.

Just like Marley, our dog sniffed at this little bundle of who-knows-what and sighed and leaned against Mark's leg to be petted and looked at us as if to say, *I can only assume you know what you're doing with this noisy, smelly thing, so I'll go along for the ride . . . just keep the biscuits coming.* And, just like in the book, I held Chelsea and sobbed as the vet inserted the drug that would end her long, adventure-filled life.

It was the day of Connor's eighth birthday. We had taken some kids to a little amusement park for some third grade–style fun, and at the end of the day, before we started dropping everyone off, Mark got a feeling he needed to swing by home and check on our then-ancient animal. Sure enough, the end was near. Poor Chelsea had suffered through several recent surgeries to remove tumors, but her health declined anyway. And on this day, she couldn't walk. She was lying in a pool of her own urine, and we couldn't stand it. Mark gently placed my sweet canine girl in the back of our SUV, and we raced to catch the vet before he left for the day. There we were in the waiting room—Mark, with a paralyzed dog in his lap; Connor, the birthday boy, who was at the height of his battle against autism, trying to comprehend what was going on; Jensen, who was seven at the time and too sleepy to be *sad*, and a handful of little kids, most of whom I'm sure we emotionally scarred for life that evening. I can hear them now: *Hey Connor, remember your eighth birthday, when we drove go-carts for a while and then your parents killed your dog?* Good times.

Mark opted to take the birthday kids home. Connor and Jensen would ride with him. I would not leave Chelsea's side. Mark rushed as fast as he could but didn't get back in time, so I was alone when Chelsea "went to sleep" for the last time.

Mark was slated to pick up Adelle in Vietnam the following week, so I was left with Connor and Jensen, my work as a staff writer on *Days*, and my grief. Thirteen and a half years later, the thought of Chelsea still makes me tear up. We've had other pets. The confused and socially ignorant pound-rescue dog, Pincus. The adorable abandoned mutt, Ace. And currently, our Vizslas, Mr. Anderson and his brother, Agent Smith. (Yes, we have watched *The Matrix* too many times.) Adelle also has her own personal pet, a never-quite-properly groomed Maltese named Carl. But up to this point, we've only had one cat.

His name was Harold. Jensen's fifth grade teacher brought a litter of cats to school one day, and Jensen had to have one. I have no recollection as to why we said yes. I don't like cats. Mark likes them even less. But Jensen got her way, and Harold soon became a very important part of the family. He was a black-and-white tuxedo cat, and he loved to roam. There was no way this guy was going to be an indoor cat. He meowed when he wanted out and meowed when he wanted in. We obeyed his every bidding. Our family was fairly nomadic for a while. We couldn't afford to buy a house because every extra dollar went to therapy for Connor. We moved four times in seven years. Harold took each move in stride, never getting lost, always finding his way home. Jensen quickly lost interest in Harold, but Adelle adroitly picked up the slack. She's an animal lover, and she adopted Harold as her own. Things ran smoothly for us cat-wise . . . for nine years.

We didn't notice anything was amiss until Harold started to lose weight. He had always been a bit of a scrapper. He was lovable when he curled up by our fireplace or on our bed, but we knew he had a ferocious side to him as well. He returned from several nocturnal outings with scars on his face or pieces of his ears missing. Harold was a fighter. And that's how he contracted AIDS.

Who knew cats could get AIDS? I didn't. But they can. And they can only give it to each other. Adelle loved Harold and was determined to sleep with him and her Maltese, Carl, and since we'd learned the facts about cat-AIDS transmission, who were we to say nay?

Harold received the best medical treatment a cat could want, and he started to do better . . . for a while. His health took a turn for the worse just as Beau arrived. Harold was starting to act a little crazy—biting and clawing at anyone who held the baby. I couldn't keep track of Beau's whereabouts and Harold's whereabouts at the same time. If Beau was in his baby swing, Harold would often be nearby, and that made me nervous. No one could predict when Harold would get a little violent. It was all too much.

I presented the problem to Adelle. She was very practical in her solution. She could see Harold's quality of life declining. She also really loved her nephew, and his safety came first. It was a horrible call for a fourteen-year-old to have to make, but she didn't hesitate. Harold had to go. It was his time.

Once that decision was made, there was no going back. I was not about to have Adelle sleep with Harold or cuddle with him one more time. If he were to go, it would be as Shakespeare wrote, "If it were done, when 'tis done, then 'twere well / It were done quickly."[2]

So Mark and I put a surprisingly willing Harold into our cat carrier, and off I went to the vet. I was surprised by my emotions. Good Lord—Adelle had already posted a "good-bye" tribute to Harold on her Facebook page, and the needle hadn't even gone in yet.

I hated doing that to him. I'd not connected to Harold the way I had with our dogs, but he had an amazingly brave spirit. He was a survivor. He'd bested raccoons, coyotes, and other free-roaming cats. But now the person he trusted most was going to send him to his death. It felt

---

2. William Shakespeare, *Macbeth*, act 1, scene 7.

so wrong, but I couldn't have him out there fighting other cats and giving them AIDS. And he couldn't stand being cooped up in the house. He was edgy and angry and sick. And there was Beau to think about. There was no other choice. But it still felt like the wrong one.

Harold always left us little presents on our doorstep. Half-eaten mice or gophers or birds. If we smelled a varmint under the house, we'd send in Harold, and he'd take care of business.

I guess he loved us in his own rough-and-tumble way. And I'm surprised to confess that I loved a cat. Harold, for what it's worth . . . I'm sorry.

Of course, I let Adelle get another cat. He's three months old, and his name is Ralphie. He has four very big cat shoes to fill.

The cat is dead. Long live the cat.

24

THE BAPTISM

There's a theological schism between Protestant baptism and Catholic christening. Jensen was brought up on one side of the schism and her husband on the other. Not a big deal . . . until the baby was born.

Jensen's husband and his family had been great about the whole religion thing. They were very observant Catholics but sweetly respected our beliefs. They were lovely about our pastor performing the wedding ceremony and only asked that a priest bless the union . . . which, now, as you know, was a wonderful idea—since that priest turned out to be the life of the party.

Jensen had been raised to believe that baptism is something you do as an adult, and Jensen had made her own choice to be baptized at the age of thirteen in our home church during a Sunday service.

I *thought* I had explained to Jensen that there was another belief system that Catholics adhere to regarding the importance of baptizing babies. Goodness! Her grandparents were Catholic. Her dad had been baptized as a baby. It wasn't that she grew up in a vacuum.

Mark and I have many friends from many different walks of faith. We have Jewish friends and Buddhist friends and friends who are just downright atheists. But apparently this melting pot of Higley diversity was lost on my oldest daughter, probably because she was playing *Sims* whenever religion was discussed. And that ignorance became startlingly apparent when things at Beau's baptism got pretty funny, pretty fast.

First off, I gave Jensen the heads-up that her in-laws were going to want their grandchild baptized . . . I mean, why wouldn't they? She nodded as I explained, and I thought all was good. Then someone gave her a christening gown for a baby shower gift, and she looked around the room confused. Why did someone give her baby boy a dress? I was out of my chair and across the room in two seconds, and I whispered in her ear, "Sorry. Forgot to give you the heads-up. Just say thank you and keep going," . . . which she did.

Once all the baby presents had been put away, I got

down to brass tacks. I clearly explained the whole infant christening deal to Jensen, and it looked like she was giving me her undivided attention. I should have checked to see if she was wearing iPod ear buds.

After the baby was born, I asked Jense if she and her husband had given any thought to who the godparents should be. As a Protestant child, I was extremely jealous of my Catholic friends who had godparents because godparents always gave the best birthday presents. I thought it was pretty cool that Beau was going to get some fairly decent presents on all of his birthdays.

Jensen said yes . . . the godparents were going to be the same people who were the best man and maid of honor from their wedding. I said: "Hold the phone . . . Your sister was the maid of honor. She can't be the godmother. She's not Catholic." Jensen assured me that she had discussed it with her husband and her in-laws and it was fine. OK . . . well, what do I know?

But I *did* know that being a godparent was about a lot more than cool gifts on your birthday. I knew that if you agreed to become a godparent, it meant that you were willing to take on the responsibility of raising this child if, God forbid, something should happen to the parents. I asked Jensen if she had run all this by Adelle, and she promised me she had.

The morning of the christening, I went into Adelle's room and saw that she was dressed in skinny jeans and a

T-shirt. While this is the typical garb of our church attend-ees, I found it highly inappropriate for the ceremony . . . especially for the godmother. But I didn't say that to her since I was no longer a helicopter mom. I just showed her the dress I was going to wear. Did she like it? Yes, she did, and she got the hint that she should change into a dress also. So she did.

We got to the chapel, and Adelle met up with her new BFF, who also just happens to be the twenty-nine-year-old brother of Jensen's husband. When this adorable young man suggested that Adelle sit with him in the front row, she thought nothing about it.

You can see where I'm going with this. Jensen *swears* she asked Adelle to be the godmother. But Adelle *swears* no one said a word to her. So when the priest asked if the godparents were willing to take on the responsibility of this child (or words to that effect), Adelle marveled at the silence. Jensen's brother-in-law nudged Adelle, who then turned and looked at me and mouthed, "Why is every-body looking at me?" That's when I knew. She had no idea. Jensen did *not* prepare her sister for this moment. Jensen just didn't see what the big deal was.

I'm not taking sides in this, but it's very possible that both Jensen and Adelle are right. Jensen probably did very *casually* mention something to Adelle, who didn't hear anything because Jensen didn't convey the significance of the whole thing . . . because . . . well, I'm not sure why.

Perhaps my informative speech to Jensen on the subject of Catholic theology should have been a multimedia event complete with a PowerPoint presentation. Maybe she only seemed to be listening to me because she was actually focusing all her attention on not vomiting (she was very pregnant at the time). It all became moot, anyway.

Adelle behaved beautifully and, once she understood what was going on, threw her hat in the ring and did all that was asked of her during the ceremony, immediately taking on the role of godmother without a hitch. Afterward, she did not back down on any of the vows she made or promises she offered while in the church. She did, however, have a few fairly intense thoughts to express to her sister about *communication*.

Adelle is going to make the best godmother. She already is awesome with the baby. She takes care of him and feeds him and does everything but change his diaper . . . a chore she simply refuses to do. She thinks dealing with fecal matter not belonging to her animals is something that should wait for her own motherhood, and since I reckon Beau will be potty-trained soon, it's no big deal. Adelle is fairly brilliant at putting up healthy boundaries, something I'm still trying to get the hang of.

Best of all, Adelle's relationship to Beau won't be about cool birthday presents (although he's totally going to get them). It's going to be about love. Because no one does love better than Adelle.

25

BOYS WILL BE BOYS

ark and I have a son, but we hadn't raised a typical little boy. We would take Connor to a birthday party when he was little and, at first, burn with envy that those three-, four-, and five-year-old little guys could talk, socialize, and have a rowdy time. Birthday parties in the greater Los Angeles area are out of control. When I was a kid we used to play pin-the-tail-on-the-donkey and eat cake. Nowadays parents hire professional entertainment. But our little Connor couldn't sit still for a magician's presentation. He couldn't focus on the funny puppet show. He was locked in his own world.

However, inevitably, halfway through the day, we'd start to notice that the high-functioning, non-autistic tykes did more whining than talking. They complained and argued. I could see moms slip into the kitchen for a second or third cocktail. The fathers, inching farther into the den, huddled with the other fathers, each dreading the moment it was time to load his cake-smeared, exhausted, annoying toddler into his prison of a car seat. That's when the screaming and the arching of the back would begin. And that's when we'd look at Connor, quietly clutching his plastic milk bottle lid (his toy of choice at the time), and secretly thank Jesus for Connor, just as he was.

Of course, Connor was not immune to tantrums. And when he threw them, he couldn't tell us why he was screaming and thrashing about. "Normal" was what we were striving for with every hour of therapy and every dollar in our checkbook. But let's face it . . . even now, as a twenty-two-year-old, Connor is himself, unique, and impossible to define. Nothing we did as parents, for or with Connor, would prepare us for what Pinocchio most yearned to be: a real, live boy.

❖ ❖ ❖

Enter Helio.

As I've mentioned previously, Helio is a dream come true. He's funny, smart, peaceful, and clever. He slipped

172

right into our family dynamic without a hiccup. But there's one thing I need to point out. He's all boy.

I had two brothers. I've had many friends of the opposite sex. I've had boyfriends. I've had one dad and one husband. I am no novice when it comes to swimming in a pool of testosterone. Boys need to do two things (until puberty, when a third is added): they need to break things and get dirty. Helio is no exception.

My son, who loves sunsets and hugs and long, quiet walks, also wants to break things and get dirty and, on occasion, has to suppress the desire to hit something or someone. Because, like it or not, boys also have an innate penchant for fighting. If you're a mom of a boy and think your son doesn't want to do those two things, go look at his stash of video games. Unless you've been a dictator about his entertainment choices—and brava for you if you have—you'll find some sort of pseudo war game in there somewhere. Also, if this weren't true, how do you explain football?

My sixteen-year-old son, Helio, took the metro from the suburbs to L.A.'s Chinatown yesterday. While riding the train, he called me to ask if he could buy fireworks. If you know anything about Southern California, you know how we suffer from wildfires. Fireworks are verboten. That doesn't mean you can't get them. It does mean you'll get busted if you are caught setting them off. I'm not talking Fourth-of-July-over-the-Hudson displays of grandeur. I'm talking crappy little sparklers and tiny cones that shoot off unimpressive fountains of lights. Most of our local kids have toyed with them from time to time . . . under close parental supervision. But I didn't think Helio should be parading around public transportation with a pocketful. So I said no.

The negotiating began . . .

"OK," he said, "how about one of those knives that you flick open?"

I gasped, "A switchblade?"

"Yeah. Those are soooooooooo cool."

"What would you do with one?"

"Uh . . . I dunno."

"Are you insane?"

"Is that a no?"

"Yes."

"OK . . . how about a taser?"

"You're kidding me, right? You're bargaining the wrong way. Every suggestion you make is getting more and more dangerous and out of the question. What are you going to ask for next, a grenade? And what makes you think you can purchase any of these things in an area of L.A. that mostly consists of restaurants and dim sum kiosks?"

"Oh, never mind."

He hung up.

Later, when I picked him up after his outing, he was sheepish. "OK, Mom, you were right. I don't know where

I got the idea Chinatown was someplace where I could get neat guy stuff."

It still amazes me that I can be right so many times with my kids and they still treat me like I don't know what the heck I'm talking about. I tried to be diplomatic and not gloat.

"Helio, I know you want to blow things up. It's my God-given job as mom to keep you from doing what billions of years of DNA is urging you to do."

"Yeah, well, I got an awesome back scratcher. So it wasn't a total waste."

Back scratcher. I can live with that.

Not long after, Helio took up mountain biking. I went on the record as being against this. I've seen Helio snowboard. He doesn't view gravity as any sort of problem. He welcomes it. Gravity is his friend. It makes him go fast and allows him to expend no energy. Uphill stinks in Helio's world. Downhill is brilliant. My opinion is that you can only live with this philosophy so long before . . . well . . . ka-boom.

I knew where this sudden passion for mountain biking came from. Helio had a girlfriend—his first. She was a world-class triathlete, which means she trained all the time. Helio did not want to be left in her literal dust.

I got in his face and said, "If you do this, you will get hurt. And if you break your pitching arm, I will personally break the other arm. DoyouunderstandwhatIamsaying?

Doyou?*Doyou?*" (I often string my sentences into one long word when speaking with Helio. Sometimes it's the only way I can get through to him.)

"Do you realize how dangerous this is? Do you have any idea, because I do, and you are going to regret this! Regret! Regret!" (Did I mention I have to repeat words in order for him to hear?)

My husband, the überboy, thought I was making way too big a deal out of all this and promptly went out and bought mountain bikes for both our sons. I was fine with Connor riding. He respects gravity. But with Helio it wasn't a case of *if;* it was a case of *when.*

My reckless son had been mountain biking a total of about six times when he came back very quietly one day. Adelle was in the kitchen with Jensen and the baby. Both girls took one look at their brother and started giggling. I didn't get it. *What's going on? What was I missing?* Helio tried to sneak over to the freezer and grab some ice, but I was like a bloodhound who had just gotten a whiff of an escaped convict. I got in his face. "Whathappened? Whatdidyoudo?" I grabbed his wrist and saw a big bump, which was growing bigger and bigger by the millisecond.

"Whatdidyoudoooooooo?"

Helio looked terrified. He looked to his sisters for support. They were too busy settling into their seats, making popcorn, and waiting for the Crazy Mom show to begin.

Mark walked in. He had actually been with Helio on the bike ride, as had Connor. Mark was unaware he was walking into a war zone. "You ready, Helio? We should probably get over to the hos . . . um . . ." Mark saw my face. Both he and Helio exchanged panicked looks. Was there a way out for them? Eh . . . no.

"Whatdidhebreak? Markareyouinsane? Wereyouwithhim? Didyouknowabouthis? Wasanyoneevergoingtotellme?"

Mark told me to calm down. It was just his wrist. It might be broken. He was about to take Helio to have it x-rayed. It was his left wrist, not his pitching arm.

Crazy Mom was unleashed. "I told you. I told you. I *told* you! Itoldyouthiswasgoingtohappen!" Helio assured me he wasn't afraid of broken bones or a cast during the summer or the hospital or needles or pain of any kind. He was just afraid of me.

"And you should be! Now you're going to miss summer baseball. Now you can't swim all summer. No swimming. No beach. Just a long, hot, *dry* summer. Happy? *Happy?* AREYOUHAPPYNOW?"

Mark stepped between the two of us and tried to calm me down with the platitude, "Lesson learned." I turned to aim my craziness at Mark. "What? What kind of philosophy is that? That's supposed to make me feel better? Trial and error? That is how my son is going to live his life? Are we going to carve that on his tombstone? 'Lesson learned'?"

I was just getting warmed up. Remember, this was the new, enlightened me. I wasn't hovering helicopter mom, but I didn't drink the man Kool-Aid either. Mark pulled Helio out of the house before I made good on my threat to break his other wrist.

Helio had the last laugh though. He came back from the hospital sporting a waterproof cast. Summer had been saved.

This week I'm starting to teach Helio how to drive. May God have mercy on my soul.

26

CONNOR'S BIG ADVENTURE

College, like everything else in my oldest son's life, has proven to be almost an overwhelming challenge. The important thing to remember is that "almost overwhelming" and "actually overwhelming" are two different things.

But clearly there was more for him to get out of life than just sitting in the confines of the four walls of a classroom. Toward the end of his junior year at Azusa Pacific University, Connor and I had a heart-to-heart. "Most of your life has been spent in therapy or school. In both those cases it's all been about you. It's time for you to get out of your own head and care about someone else."

After a little digging around and prayer for God to guide us, Connor and I decided that it would be a great adventure and good for his personal growth for him to spend a summer in the Czech Republic working with a group called Young Life, ministering to teens in that geographically beautiful but somewhat emotionally bleak country.

Still reeling from the effects of Communism, the Czech people seemed to be very open to Americans coming and doing the whole cross-cultural thing. I'm not one of those people who thinks the whole world has to think and act like Americans. I love and embrace other cultures, and Connor was just there to embrace the Czech lifestyle and offer them a chance to meet someone from the United States. If Connor got the chance to share his faith with them, so much the better. If not, connection between people is always a good thing. Also, it would be a chance for Connor to live in a world where language would not be a barrier. I know that sounds strange—going to a foreign country to avoid language problems—but as you now know, verbal processing has always been a trial for him. Now he could be with people whom he wouldn't understand anyway, autism or no, so he wouldn't have to stress about not being understood. Even if he made friends who did speak English, syntax and content wouldn't be issues. Connor could experience a kind of social freedom he'd never felt before, free from the constraints of auditory confusion. It was too good an opportunity to miss.

He could practice getting out of his head and empathizing with others, and he could do it without words.

So off he went for a summer abroad. But it wasn't his finest time away from home.

Connor spent his freshman year of college in Florida. That was the hardest good-bye I've ever endured. I watched Mark and Connor drive off in Connor's convertible Mustang and head cross-country. Mark called me a few days later with a catch in his voice. He had just left Connor at his apartment at Beacon College in Leesburg, Florida, looking as lost and forlorn as he had that first day of kindergarten.

I hung up the phone, and my knees turned to Jell-O. I couldn't breathe. I was out shopping but had to find a place to sit down or I'd pass out. I'd comforted myself during the initial days of my son's absence with the thought that at least he was with his dad. But now he was alone, thousands of miles away. What if he needed me? How long would it take to get to him? He was such a homebody. How would he handle living with three other guys in a two-bedroom apartment? He'd never had to share a bedroom before. I thought about the lovely, dark, and peaceful "time-out" room that he had in his special preschool. It was a special place for him to chill out when he experienced sensory overload. Would he be able to find such a place now?

Of course, he survived just fine. He wasn't happy during his time in Florida, but he didn't die either. I was so proud of him when he got back on the plane and headed east after winter break. He so badly didn't want to go back. We knew several freshmen at other schools that year who didn't go back and finish their freshman years. But Connor did. He had trouble with his roommates and trouble with his classes and hated being so far from home. But he's no quitter. He made it through the first year with passing grades.

That summer, he felt he was ready to take on the challenge of a "real" college. Beacon was a great place, and we believed in their mission to make the college experience available to kids with learning disabilities. But Connor'd had enough. He wanted to be fully integrated in college with "regular" students just the way he'd been in elementary school and high school. We were so proud of him when he was accepted to Azusa Pacific University. It's a great Christian liberal arts school, and he reunited there with some kids he'd gone to high school with.

At the end of his junior year, it was a given that he was on the slow track. He wasn't going to graduate in four years. But then neither had I; neither had Mark . . . lots of students haven't and won't. So it was no big deal when he decided to take the whole summer off. No school, no therapy, no autism.

Once again, Mark was game to go along. He traveled with Connor to Ostrava, Czech Republic, and helped Connor settle in for a summer of camp counseling, mountain bike riding, and making new friends. Mark left him in the care of a wonderful Czech family until the apartment that had been arranged for him was ready.

I remember when I went to Germany my sophomore year at Pepperdine. I was away from home at the age of eighteen, but I was with a bunch of my friends; Connor was doing the abroad thing . . . but doing it alone. His trip to Europe would be far different from the one I had taken thirty years earlier. For one thing, we could talk all the time. Connor bought a disposable, prepaid cell phone. We also had Skype. This was amazing. All I had when I was away from home was the good ol' mail. I got one phone call from my parents the whole year I was gone. Modern technology was going to make things a lot easier for Connor. Or so I thought.

So there he went. And actually, it wasn't all we'd hoped for.

As you probably surmised by now, this isn't the kind of book where problems are presented and solved all in nice, neat packages. Life is messy. Our family is messy. And as it turned out, Connor's trip to the Czech was very messy.

He tried very hard to fit in. His attempts were misunderstood and judged by other leaders and parents of the kids he was there to lead. I don't want to go into too much detail because this is my story, not his, but we tried something and it wasn't a good fit. The old me would have called it a disaster. But now I know we're all just on a journey. It's OK to throw up a white flag every once in a while. Connor's a great guy—no doubt about it. And he's not very different from everyone else. We all start down a path . . . and then you have to backtrack and go back, push the reset button and start again. He learned a lot on the trip, and learning isn't always comfortable.

In the old days, pre-wedding, I probably would have really freaked out over this. But I didn't, and neither did Mark. We realized the great European experiment of 2011 had gone awry, and it was time to pull the plug. So we brought Connor home after just a few weeks.

The experience wasn't a failure or a mistake. It was (as my father loves to say) what it was. When I was younger, I'd hate when he'd say that, because kids have so little life experience that they don't understand profoundly simple statements. But I've thrown that phrase (*It is what it is*) up against the wall more than a few times in my life, and like well-cooked spaghetti, it always seems to stick. Connor's trip was what it was. And it's up to him to learn from it or not. Meanwhile, Mark and I patted ourselves on the back, proud that one of our kids had (what could be construed as) a setback and neither of us ended up in a hospital, insane asylum, or morgue. Progress at last.

I love what Anne Lamott said in her book *Traveling Mercies*:

> I don't know why life isn't constructed to be seamless and
> safe, why we make such glaring mistakes, things fall so

short of our expectations and our hearts get broken and our kids do scary things and our parents get old and don't always remember to put pants on before they go out for a stroll. I don't know why it's not more like it is in the movies, why things don't come out neatly and lessons can't be learned when you're in the mood for learning them, why love and grace often come in such motley packaging.[3]

This was such a lesson for me. As usual, Connor taught me more than anyone else in my life. His trip wasn't a failure. But what if it was? So what? Failure is just a word. Sometimes we say it; sometimes we think it. Then we shrug it off and move on.

For Connor, it's on to the next challenge . . . the next adventure. When a little time passes, I'm sure he will look back at all that happened during his sojourn in Europe and take pride in the friends he made and the self-reliance he learned. He will also be honest and admit that perhaps there were a few situations he could have avoided altogether. And as he plows through his senior year of college, he'll be a better person for his time in Europe. My oldest son is a person of endless possibilities. And lately I've been noticing . . . I mean, I think . . . That is to say . . . I believe he's on the brink of . . . well, I'm not sure what. But I'm smart enough to recognize a "brink" when I see one.

---

3. Ann Lamott, *Traveling Mercies* (New York: Pantheon, 1999), 143–44.

27

DEAR CHRISTOPHER, . . .

I haven't seen you in so long. How are you doing? Your mom showed me pictures of you, but I haven't actually gotten to give you a big hug in ages. Be that as it may, you are never far from my thoughts. Knowing you will always be one of the highlights of my life.

I remember when I first met you at Villa Esperanza sixteen years ago. Wasn't that a wonderful school? One of the first of its kind—specifically designed for kids like you and Connor . . . autistic kids. You and Connor were both five. Neither of you could speak. But both of you enjoyed school. You were friends.

Then your life took a very different turn—a different

direction than that of Connor's. There were no first words for you. You didn't like to look at people much, or look around much. There weren't a whole lot of things in your life to grab your attention.

Your body felt adrift, lost with all the air around you. You preferred to have something on your head, squeezing it, holding it all in. You liked having something around your wrist, hugging it, making you feel secure and safe. There's nothing wrong with either of those things.

Do you know how wonderful you are? I think you do. Do you know you have the best parents in the world? Your mom is one of the greatest people I've ever met. She never wanted to be a saint; she just wanted to be a mom. Your older brother just wanted to be a brother. And your dad just wanted to be a dad. But there is no "just" with you. You took them to a place of great emotion, great love, great fear. But aren't we all afraid of something? Afraid that the world won't turn out the way we want it to? There's nothing wrong with that either. As long as love is stronger than fear. And it is with your family. I don't really know very many people who are loved as much as you are.

Now you're a grown man. And still, you have no words to express yourself. No eye contact. Not only do you need to have your head and your arms squeezed, but you've added style with a towel you constantly and jauntily sport around your neck.

You love to be in the kitchen, cooking. The smells are so real to you—the touch of each different kind of food on your fingertips. Everything that I take for granted about food, you relish. You fix food with your mom, then deliver delicious gourmet meals to businesses in the neighborhood. What a cool job you have. You don't need words to be an ambassador of friendship . . . just yummy chow.

What are you thinking when you go out on your delivery route? All these people, Christopher, running around, trying to buy bigger houses and faster cars—so many people full of hate, full of anger, full of desperation. But not you. You are pure. You are holy. You are love.

If I ever speak blithely of autism when it comes to Connor, please know I don't want to, in any way, disrespect the life you and your family have carved out for yourselves. We all walk a separate path. Connor's is Connor's and yours is yours. Neither of you is more blessed or more loved by God than the other. It's just different. You taught me that. And (not to make this all about me, but it is *my* book) I'm a better person for knowing you. When we get to heaven, we will finally get to have that chat I've been dying to have with you (no pun intended). And at last I will get to hear all those wonderful thoughts you've been having for so many years, clearly and beautifully articulated.

I can't wait.

28

EVERYTHING OLD
IS NEW AGAIN

I just got back from the Pasadena Rite Aid where I purchased a retinol-based, age-resistant eye cream and some diapers. When I told Adelle what I'd bought, she asked if the diapers were for me. Ha-flippin'-ha. No. They were for the baby.

The thing about having a baby in my life now is that it brings home one of the major revelations of my life. Stylistically speaking, I'm just now peaking.

When I was a little tap-dancing, preschool-age doll, I was adorable. I have the pictures to prove it. But when I hit elementary school, I went through what I would like to generously call my awkward phase, and it lasted all the way through my sophomore year of high school. I finally got a little break my junior and senior years. I guess if you're going to get a two-year reprieve from an awkward phase, the last two years of high school are a great time to do it. As a junior and senior at Valhalla High School in El Cajon, California, I was a cheerleader and had a boyfriend and did all the fun stuff all-American teens get to do. I was one of the "good girls" who didn't put out, do drugs, or drink. Back then there really was a class system in school. Now, from what I can tell, there are no "good" kids and "bad" kids. There are just kids. Drinking and drugs are the sad default mode of their generation.

If you've got high school students who aren't succumbing to the overwhelming pop culture message that you can do whatever feels good whenever you like, then good for you. But you've got to know, that's not the norm . . . not anymore. As you know from my sojourn with Jensen, I learned this the hard way. So did my younger kids . . . I hope. Anyway, being in high school for *me* in the mid-seventies meant there were drugs around, but not around me. I had placed myself in a group where there was just none of that available. I never had to turn down anything because I was never offered anything.

I must have placed myself in a similar category in college. After I graduated, one of my friends talked about going through his cocaine phase. I drew a blank. "When was that?" He laughed, "Oh, it lasted about three years, but we never did it in front of you, Dena. You're a good girl."

Hmmm . . . I guess that was a good thing . . . considering the hospital incident I would have later in life.

How did I get on this subject? Oh yeah, *peaking*.

When I was growing up, almost all my girlfriends were much prettier than I was. And I'm not being falsely modest here. Once again, I have the photos to prove it. I learned early on to be funny and clever and make my way up the ladder of success that way. All in all, it's a great way. But now, the strangest thing has happened. My grandson has given me a new perspective on my looks. Oh sure, my crow's feet continue to deepen, and gravity is having its way with me. But because I get to wear the GRANDMA sash over my clothes (à la Miss America), it's all jaunty and jejune. I confess I love taking the baby to the grocery store or to a restaurant or anywhere public. He's such a beautiful baby, and everyone comments on how amazing he is and how lucky I must be to have such a gorgeous baby. This is where I get to say my line: "I'm not his mommy; I'm his grandmother." And if I don't have the baby with me, I simply show pictures of my grandchild so I still get to say my line.

I'm pretty small and basically physically fit for someone old enough to remember the *first* time go-go boots were hip. So I'll be able to climb the jungle gym and trees with Beau and hike and do all kinds of active stuff for a good long while. Something about this season of my life is making me feel young. And it's not just Beau. Thanks to Adelle and Helio, I dabble in Teenspeak. I know what *wez* means and that getting *yolked up* has nothing to do with eggs, and, although I'm not fluent, I know that *sick* is good and to *chuck up the deuce* means to flash a peace sign. I'm not going to giggle about this, but it does make me feel current.

I was in Trader Joe's the other day. The clerk asked me if I'd found everything I needed. I immediately improvised a whole stand-up routine: what did I really *need* in life and—as well stocked as their shelves are—did the store offer things people *needed*? Then I confessed to this clerk that I went into his store only searching for a few goodies and then fell in love with some impulse items that I instantly had to have. But did that really constitute need? (Don't worry; no one was behind me. I wasn't holding up the line.) After my routine was done, the clerk clapped his hands and exclaimed, "You're fun!"

Really? I was fun, not just funny? How fantastic is that? It especially feels good after coming out of a long stint of the doldrums. But what's even greater than that is that I appear to actually physically look better to people. And I think it's just because I feel better. One (quite elderly) waiter actually told me I was cute the other day. I am many things, but cute is not one of them, so he may have had eyesight problems. But I'll take the compliment. I haven't heard that word since I was three.

I know my husband thinks I'm "dorbs" (Adelle's shorthand for adorable). But total strangers? I can't get enough of this little scenario that's playing out over and over in my life. I know it's terribly shallow of me. But I don't care. It won't last long. I'm sure the AARP version of my awkward phase is just around the corner. So I'm enjoying this while I can. And it's all because I'm a happy, grateful grandma. Thank you, Adelle. Thank you, Helio. And thank you, Beaudon.

29

SPEAKING OF BEING A WORKING GRANDMOTHER...

After my epiphany with Beaudon and my realization that once again I was running myself ragged trying to be a Grandmaholic, I took time to slow down, stopped trying to log too many hours with the baby, and focused on the kids I had at home as well as my career. I finally found a nice balance where I really hit my stride at work.

Remember, the ratings had settled into a new low that was troubling, but I had an upcoming story I believed in and an amazing team who made it all click. I felt good about what I saw on the air and felt good about what we were creating in the writers' room. I felt invigorated creatively. I felt strong. I felt in control.

And that's when I was fired.

Why? I'm not sure, but I have a few guesses. I can't say it totally came out of the blue. There were warning signs, to be sure. The Suits and I did not agree on many things, but I'm a creative person by nature and confident in my instincts. At the same time I'm humble enough to not insist things go "my way or the highway." I assumed that out of our conflict would come the best story possible. It was all about process for me. Apparently, not everyone shared my love of process.

I have to also factor in the cancellation of two ABC soaps. Never in the history of daytime television had two shows been canceled at the same time. Panic ensued, and *Days* was not immune.

When the *Titanic* sank, people behaved with calm courage. Not that I'm making a literal connection here, but if *Days* was the *Titanic*, people would be pushing others into the water, and rowboats would capsize as stark terror overtook those flailing about in the water. No one would have been saved.

I was the first of many firings. A guillotine was figuratively set up, and the lopping off of heads began. First mine. Then our brilliant executive producer. Then three of my staff writers. Then another producer and a total of six contracted actors. All these people, in my humble opinion, are the best in the business. And now, with only four daytime shows left, the possibilities of any of us working on a soap again is grim at best.

Strangely, I'm very relieved. Soaps are doomed anyway. Soon there will be nothing on daytime TV but talk shows, food shows, and reruns of old movies. Oh, and telenovelas.

I saw this course change coming and started to work on Plan B long before I was let go. Yes, this book is part of plan B, but it didn't start out that way. I started writing it a year before I was fired just to get a few things off my chest. Now, well, I need a new career.

I hold no grudges. Although I was very sad that my dear friend of twenty-six years called me up and told me he was making a change. He actually said it like that—like he was talking to a total stranger. I guess it's easier to fire a stranger than a friend. I hung up the phone numb from the shock of it all. I mean, I knew I was going to be out of a job eventually, but I wasn't expecting it so soon. It's like knowing death is coming, but instead of peacefully floating away in your sleep at the age of ninety-seven, you're hit by a bus in the prime of your life. Or, if another metaphor is useful, coming up too fast from the sea floor to the surface totally gave me the bends.

I had to detox. It's not much of an exaggeration to say I went through the d.t.'s. I got the call on a Wednesday. I had just finished editing two shows. I had also just completed a long story document. I was in the thick of it. I was clicking on all cylinders. I was taking phone calls and dashing off e-mails, and thirty fictional characters were roaming about in my head, so I was never alone. And then, in an instant . . . it was all gone.

For two weeks, I didn't know what to do with myself. Not only had I enjoyed the fast pace of soaps, but I adored my team of writers. They were my friends. This was my family, my community. I would always have them as friends, but we wouldn't gather around a table three times a week and make each other laugh, finish each other's sentences, and keep tabs on all the running jokes we had going any longer. I missed everything about my job. I was bereft. I was grieving. I was at a loss.

My low point came when I sat in front of the TV and let ice cream dribble down my shirt. I didn't get up to change. I didn't throw it in the wash so it wouldn't stain. I just sat there watching Steve Martin movies. (When I'm psychotic, I go through actor obsessions. My last one was Tom Hanks.) My kids gave me a wide berth and let me go through the emotional stages of death: denial, anger, bargaining, depression, and acceptance.

I organically followed those exact steps, and slowly all the agony and depression were replaced with the growing sense of peace. My cell phone stopped ringing. My e-mail didn't pile up. My shoulders relaxed. The strain of trying to keep a dying show afloat was no longer there. My appetite came back. The career I'd built for twenty-six years was over. After much thrashing about, I was OK.

Having a little distance from the drama of it all, I'm starting to question the validity of the genre at all. I'm growing sick and tired of our pop culture's obsession with emotions. In fact, I recently heard a TV personality wax on about how all of us are not the sum total of our thoughts but of our feelings.

Sorry, but my feelings don't define me, and anyone who has had a teenage daughter knows that she most certainly is not defined by her feelings, which change daily, hourly, minute by minute.

In fact, I'm starting to conclude that many of the problems our society faces today are because we spend way too much time talking about our feelings. How are you feeling today? How am I feeling today? How does that make you feel? These are all pointless questions. Instead, why isn't anyone asking: Separate and apart from your feelings, what is the one great truth of your life? What are your goals? What does common decency tell you to do in a crisis? How do you treat your fellow man? No one is asking these questions, and the storylines and rhetoric of soap operas wasn't helping much. On *Days* we were all about feelings. As I wrote before, I adored our matriarch, Alice Horton, but at some point it really started to bug me that the writers were always having her advise people to "follow your heart." That's terrible advice. The Bible says, "The heart is deceitful above all things" (Jer. 17:9). And, "Above all else, guard your heart, for it is the wellspring of life" (Prov. 4:23). Now, that sounds like the truth to me. In my own life, my heart has deceived me over and over again. I had always gotten into trouble when I hadn't guarded my heart against the world, against itself. But you never heard that kind of talk on a soap.

"I love you." "I hate you." Blah, blah, blah. I'd written about every feeling a person could possibly feel. Feelings are just feelings, not facts. But that's not what you hear from the characters in soaps. On my journey to self-realization, I discovered that I was a part of a pop-culture machine that was feeding the ethical void of our world, and I wasn't comfortable with my contribution.

I have no regrets. Life is a process. I'm glad for the time I spent as a daytime television writer, but I don't think, in good conscience, I could be one now. Yes, I was pushed out of the nest, but God works in mysterious ways.

Ouch. That's a horrible cliché.

But that doesn't make it any less true.

30

DEEP STUFF

I hold no degree in any field of psychology. I have never studied child development. But I am a mom of four kids. And I think that makes me one heck of an expert.

My hat is off to all moms of kids with special needs. I have been dropped facedown on the floor by the sheer acts of love I have seen displayed by the mothers I've met who have kids with the big A or CP or MD or CF or . . . a thousand other disorders in the big alphabet soup of disease in this world.

My friend Joni has been an advocate for such kids for as long as I've known her. In case you don't know anything about Joni, she's been a quadriplegic her whole adult life. She's turned her disability into a platform for reform. She's taught me so much. Living with a disability is like being forced down to the lower depths of the ocean. You don't want to swim there, because the pressure builds and it's hard to breathe and dark and frightening. But it also exposes you to a whole world of beauty. The coral, the fish, the amazing teeming life all around you. You long to just paddle on the surface of the water, but you can't. So while you're down there, you might as well make the most of it. That's what Joni did best. Can I just tell you about one amazing Spirit-filled moment I shared with Joni?

We were sitting outside during a break at a women's retreat. Connor was about seven at the time and really had no speech. I told Joni that I often had dreams that little Connor could talk to me. I asked her if, in her dreams, she could walk. She hadn't walked since she was a teenager, and that was many years ago. Instead of answering me, Joni asked me the most amazing question: was I *surprised* in my dream that Connor could talk?

This was so long ago. I wish I could tell you the answer I gave her, but I can't. I remember the dreams, but I can't remember the answer. The reason her question was so important is that she was asking if my subconscious was grieving Connor's autism. I don't know if she knows how profound her question was. I don't think she did . . . or does. But it was. And now it's moot, since Connor can now communicate just fine. But back in the day when God gave me access to someone as Spirit-filled and amazing as Joni, I was lost. I needed an answer. And here's what she said to me: "I don't know what to tell you, Dena. But here's what I *can* tell you. I don't recall having dreams of being able to walk. But I do have dreams of being able to swim. It's not as if I'm swimming now. I've been given visions of a pool of gold in heaven. I'm diving in and swimming my heart out. My body is working perfectly."

That one brief conversation changed my life. Joni's accident happened while she was swimming. What kind of amazing spiritual symmetry is that? Her answer to me was clearly God's answer to me. And here's what I heard from God Himself:

I'm not going to give you any promises or assurances in this life, Dena. I'm just going to tell you what you already know. Joni will walk in heaven. Connor will talk in heaven. And, Dena, you won't be a demanding butthead in heaven. (I might be paraphrasing that last bit.)

OK. I got it. Our wounds in this life matter to the eternal God. But we will be more than compensated when we are living with God. God spoke through Joni that day. And although Connor did learn to talk, I was forced to walk by faith for a very long time. I wanted promises, but God gave me grace.

I asked for a vision of Connor's imminent future. God gave me a vision of his ultimate future. And that's what

I really needed. If we don't believe in an eternal afterlife, how can we possibly raise children with any sort of wisdom or hope? This world can be a pretty bleak place. Without hope it would be unbearable. The best legacy you can pass on to your kids is hope.

31

CLOSURE

Strangely, right before I was let go from my job as head writer of *Days of Our Lives*, I was nominated for an Emmy. Last time I was nominated, I won. So did Mark. It was for our work on *One Life to Live*. I was the head writer there for almost three years, and Mark was a dialogue writer. We were fired before the Emmy voting took place, and I didn't attend the awards show.

So this year, even though I'd been fired, I was going to go. They were holding the event in Las Vegas, and I asked Adelle to be my date. She happily agreed, and we were both eager to connect with my writing team buddies, catch up, and just have a good time.

But I *had* been fired. There were bound to be awkward moments. So I planned my Vegas strategy carefully.

Adelle and I slipped into town Friday night. We zipped to the hotel where everyone from NBC, ABC, and *SOD* (*Soap Opera Digest*) were staying. Reporters, actors, producers, directors . . . I did not want to run into any of these people.

On Saturday I arranged to have a private cabana in the furthermost corner of the furthermost pool. Adelle and I had the best day. We played cards, read books, and just hung out with each other. It was a fun girls' day. But as the day progressed, I could feel a change in the air. "They" were arriving. I couldn't see them, but I knew they were out there, getting closer and closer . . . descending on the town.

I had no worries about running into *them* in the casino. I don't gamble. But just walking from the pool to the elevators was enough to make me break out in a cold sweat. Why was I being so neurotic? No one was going to physically attack me. At least, I didn't think so. I was being ridiculous, and I knew it. I was hiding out from people who were nice. People I should seek out and reconnect with. I just couldn't. My paranoia grew and grew. Whenever I had to traverse from one area of the resort to another, I felt like Bugs Bunny sneaking around on tiptoes. I even went so far as to walk behind large families, trying to blend in, to look like part of a group. What a nut job I was!

My hypervigilance paid off. I only saw a handful of pre-picked friends before the event. On Sunday afternoon, Adelle and I got dressed to the nines, did our hair and makeup, and then I headed down to the lobby alone to arrange for transport to the awards show.

There they all were. A big gaggle of actors—pretty much everyone I'd been trying to avoid for the better part of three days. The minute I rounded the corner and saw them, I stopped dead in my tracks. *Should I go back? I can't. I've been spotted. OK, stay calm. Act nonchalant . . . as if it's the most perfectly natural thing in the world for their defunct ex–head writer to walk among them. Not awkward at all.*

Awkward. Horribly awkward.

Then "he" stepped up.

My friend and my NBC mentor opened his arms and welcomed me. He hugged on me and gave me all the love I needed to face anyone and anything that night.

I'm so socially uncomfortable and hate to go out in public even under normal circumstances, but in this case, I was downright freaked. The press hadn't been kind to me in the last days. *Days* hadn't been kind to me in the press. I'd read bad stuff. And from the looks on the actors' faces, they'd read stuff too. Then God provided me with, not one angel, but two. My favorite network Suit stayed close and chatted with me until my amazing Adelle entered. Who could not want to be with Adelle? She was magnificent.

She transcended age and inexperience, exuded lovely confidence. She was stately and regal and so beautiful. My fifteen-year-old daughter worked the room, air-kissed everyone, chatted it up, was socially graceful, and I was free to be my lame self.

We all boarded a shuttle and headed to the Hilton, where the awards were to take place. And that's where the lovefest began.

So many of the actors on the show actually sought me out to tell me how much they'd appreciated what I'd written for them. How stupid was I for worrying? In the end, it didn't matter. No, I didn't win. But I did have a wonderful time with my daughter. And my friends were there and people (actors included) who actually told me to my face that they appreciated my work. So I came away a winner.

32

THE TRUTH ABOUT TRUTH

think almost everyone starts off building a family with the belief that eventually they will hit stride. The kids will be healthy and happy, and love and respect will flow. My friend Karen always believed that as a person gets older and wiser, life will become easier, require less effort. I shared that assumption. Now both Karen and I realize that we never really do find our rhythm in this life, and getting through it all is always going to require an exhausting amount of effort.

Once you realize a goal is unattainable, I think it's important to change your goal. Otherwise you just grow old, frustrated, and dissatisfied. So here's my new goal: to be armed with faith, wisdom, and a sense of humor so I can tackle whatever comes my way.

I no longer dream of a smooth, easy path for my children. I pray for them to be tough, resilient, and empathetic. I can't bulldoze ahead of them and clear away the debris of the future. Nor should I want to. It's how we face adversity, not success, that defines us. I haven't always handled success very well. Success, of any flavor or degree, is a slippery slope. I have tended to drop my guard and get spiritually lazy and more than a little self-centered during my brief bouts of success, both in my private life and in my career. I've only handled the difficult seasons with a little better attitude . . . a little more balance. A very little . . .

I just don't do well with *well*. Now that I know that, I'm hoping to do better with *better*. I think it would be crazy to not want our lives to constantly get better. It's just my definition of *better* that needs tweaking. I used to think *better* was more stuff, more holidays, and more quiet. Now things are better if my kids are overcoming, striving, accepting challenges, and displaying grace under pressure. *Better* for my marriage means honoring my husband, even in the midst of our disagreements . . . and feeling honored in return. *Better* in my marriage means I've retired my wagging finger and my explosive temper.

So now that I've got new goals, how can I visualize my future? What does all this *better* look like? I don't know. I'm not even sure I'll recognize it when it occurs.

Fortunately I have wise people in my life who are sure to point out *better* for me when it arrives, should it escape my attention. I especially have to give a shout-out to my girlfriends. There is a trio of amazing women in my life who have lifted me up when I couldn't stand on my own, who've wrapped their arms around me when I've felt alone, who charted a course for me when I'd lost my way. If you're a woman and a mom and you try to do life without girlfriends, you'll never make it. They are essential! I would not be breathing today without my beloved "sistahs." There is just no way. So to those few brave souls—Jackie, Tami, and Karen, you know who you are— thank you. And to the women in my family who have walked the mom-path before me (Myrtle, Hester, and Carol), thank you for being my inspiration. Life is hard enough without throwing mother challenges into the mix, but the women in my family who've done it all before (in much more difficult circumstances) managed beautifully.

Each generation has its unique parenting challenges. Perhaps previous generations put on too brave a face at the expense of internal examination or relational bonding. While the emerging generation seems to do very little but stare in fascination at their own navels night and day. Where does that put us? What are we to do? Where do I find *better*?

Well, like my mother and her mother before and her mother before her, I know where to look for it.

On my knees.

33

MEN

*T*his book is not meant to be exhaustive on the subject of child rearing. But I *am* championing overworked mothers, so the subject of where-is-dad must come up. I have thought of four possible scenarios (once again, not exhaustive).

Number one category: The father is just as much mired in this over-parenting mess as the mom. They coach all their kids' teams, or rush home from work to drive them to all their practices and sit in the stands watching not only all the games but all the *practices* as well. They volunteer to lead committees, booster boards, etc. They stay up and wait for their kids to come home from dates and offer hours of unsolicited advice.

If you separate all these attributes, none of them are bad. Taken individually all of them are good. But when you bunch them together, mix them up, it gets tricky. When do men cross that line from good to too much? I'll leave that for you to decide.

Group two is the father who is there but isn't there. He brings home the bacon and leaves the child rearing to the mom. He asks the kids how their day went at school but doesn't really listen to the answer.

Group three consist of fathers who want to help but it seems they can never do anything right. I see dads at the grocery story on their cell phones with panic in their voices as they ask their wives: Did you want the gluten-free crackers or the regular kind? Poor guy. He knows if he gets it wrong there will be heck to pay.

My husband has spent some time in category #1 but spends most of his time these days in this last category. He chauffeurs kids quite often, but their schedules are so crazy sometimes he'll pick them up in the front when they come out the back or there will be an unexpected half day at school and no one told him.

Am I kind to him? No. I snap: Just let me handle it. What a witch.

We have found it best to divide and conquer. Mark will take on full responsibility for one area of our children's activities and I take another. That way there is very little miscommunication. If we need help with our share of the burden, a text or an e-mail is much better than a verbal communication. Adding technology can avoid the "I told you"/"No, you didn't" argument that no one wins unless you have a time machine . . . in which case, can I borrow it?

Then there is a fourth category that I have heard of but, like Atlantis or the Loch Ness monster, I have never seen. This category consists of husbands (and wives) that just do everything right. If you're in this category, stop reading. Why have you read this far? Why did you even pick up this book in the first place? Really. Stop. There's just no point in finishing the last two chapters of this book. I have nothing to offer you. Nothing.

34

ARE YOU IN THE CLUB?

I find myself in a strange holding pattern in my career. I'm living off of my contract payoff from *Days*, and I've sold this book but it hasn't hit the shelves yet. So I'm just taking care of the kids, taking a few classes, and trying to learn how to better understand myself and . . . um . . . did I mention taking care of the kids?

I've had one of those days. Things went along swimmingly for me until school got out at 3:05. It was then that a driving marathon began for Helio and Adelle that did not end until nine at night when I went to pick up Adelle from piano and found out the building owners had turned off all the lights and locked her and her piano teacher inside the building. Say what? That's enough of the nine o'clock at night stuff. I have to reshuffle a few things so I can get her out of there before *even the musicians* have quit. That means moving tutoring to a different time, and that means moving her track workouts and moving her physical therapy and . . . you get the idea.

I keep putting up healthy boundaries, but people and kids keep trying to knock them down. But I stand firm. I tell the kids and their friends that I would be a first-class hypocrite if I didn't practice what I have written in my book. So I do . . . even though it may not make me the most popular person in town.

The more attempts I make to live my life free of guilt or exhaustion, the more I see that it's a very tricky message that I preach. But I stand more convicted than ever that a revolution must take place.

If we moms realize our limits and admit them freely to our friends and neighbors, teachers and coworkers, then they eventually will get the message. And if we turn down one or two requests for our time, no PTA boards will fold; no schools will shut down. Don't buy into the notion that the situation is dire or that lives are at stake. Actually, lives *are* at stake. The lives of good moms who need to just chill. If George Washington and Donald Trump could succeed without their moms driving them to ten extracurricular activities every day, then by golly, so can our kids.

As I've started to verbally share the content of my book with friends, I've been surprised to hear how many of them instantly relate. One woman told me that her son, at age thirteen, freaked out one night as he was being shuttled from one lesson to another, tugged at his hair and screamed: is this how the rest of my life is going to be?

Other women tilt their heads, arms akimbo, as they soak in the message. Could it be possible? Is there such a thing as a calm household? A calm mom? Do they have the right to set personal boundaries? After I assure them that it is all true, they open up, share with me that they are barely hanging on—literally at their wits' end as to how to juggle work and kids or how to deal with a grown child in the house. And even stranger than that, they ask me for advice.

This is dicey. I shouldn't be an advice giver. I have no degree or qualifications in this area. But that doesn't keep me from being opinionated. So I usually say something like this, "Make him get a job." And while moms love this advice, it doesn't always go over big with kids. Or even with some other adults.

One evening I was bemoaning the fact that my son doesn't really know the value of a dollar. It was at this point in the conversation that the woman with whom I was speaking said she never wanted her kids to work for minimum wage—they shouldn't set their sights that low.

I don't even know what to do with this comment. It

doesn't make sense to me. I think young men and women should all work for minimum wage at one time or another and understand that any labor no matter how humble is worthy of their maximum effort. Hard work is to be embraced, not avoided. Sometimes the harder the better. Frankly, in this economy, any job is of value. And isn't it a dangerous notion to teach our kids they're too good for something? Our kids need to be humble and grateful. Hard work never hurt anyone. I washed dishes, floors, and a lot of other non-fun stuff in the various jobs I've held—and it was ALL a great experience for me. My time making milkshakes and flipping burgers at the local Dairy Queen inspired me to even higher ambitions than ever before. If I hadn't been grounded early on—getting some of that character I was complaining about earlier, I think I would have folded up my mommy-tent when the road got rough. I may not be the world's greatest mom, but I've never given up. I love my kids—and crazy or sane, I'll always be their mom. However, I prefer sane.

I was picking up Adelle from physical therapy the other day, and there was a woman standing at the check-in desk having a full-on, psychotic breakdown. I've had many myself, so she had my sympathy almost immediately.

"No!" she screamed. "My daughter's session is today. TODAAAAAYYYY! It couldn't have been yesterday. She had a doctor's appointment yesterday. You have to take her today. YOUHAVETOOOOO!!!"

I so wanted to step in and assure this woman that surely it would all work out one way or another. If her daughter really needed physical therapy, someone would take her, appointment or no. And that's basically what the receptionist said. But the mom was on another wavelength. She needed to be *right* about the appointment time. She insisted someone *apologize* to her for *their* mistake. I wanted to invite her to sit down with me, have a stick of gum, and take a little mommy time-out. I wanted to make her understand that, while being RIGHT might seem important in the moment, nothing was worth coming unglued and screaming at a poor, young, blonde girl who continually stared at a computer screen that clearly displayed living proof that yesterday was the appointment day, and not today. I wanted to give this mother a hug. But I didn't. She obviously wasn't in a huggy mood. But it was a good reminder for me. Ahh, the good ole days, where I was always one missed appointment away from a straitjacket.

35

THE TEST

So, dear overburdened reader, what advice do I have for you besides, *Tell your teens to get a job*? I guess, first of all, we have to identify your parenting style. In the world of addiction, they say, "The first step is to admit that you have a problem." So? Are you a Momaholic? If you're not sure, here's a simple quiz you can take. I based all these questions on my own past mistakes . . . or what I now view as mistakes.

Have you done any of these things in the last week?

1) Did you perform more than one fetch-and-carry errand per child per day? (This includes

taking anything to them at school that they have forgotten. This also includes carrying their backpacks for them at *any* time.)

2) Did you go clothes shopping with one of your kids and lugged their items around the store for them? (Don't laugh; this was a hard habit for me to break.)

3) Do you allow your kids' friends to call you by your first name? (This is not a hard-and-fast rule; it's more a style choice. It's just hard to get respect once one of your kid's nine-year-old friends calls out to you, *Hey Betsy! Wassup?*)

4) Do you EVER ask one of your kids if he or she is mad at you? (Once again, this was something I used to do . . . a lot.)

5) Do you ever cross the line from helping with homework to just flat-out doing it? You know the line I'm talking about; don't pretend you don't.

6) Have you ever been called to school by the vice principal because one of your kids is in trouble and you made an excuse for your child's bad behavior?

7) Have you let your teen slack off because he or she is tired? I've got news for you. Your teenager is not tired. Anyone over the age of thirteen and under the age of thirty should never be tired no matter what is going on . . . seriously. If young men, not much older than your teen, could spend countless

sleepless nights on a transport boat and then storm the beaches at Normandy, surely your teenager can weather a few late nights before finals without drama. And have you noticed how your exhausted teen perks up when a last-minute party invite comes along? Food for thought.

8) Speaking of food: have you ever made two (or more) different entrées for dinner, trying to please everyone, and allowed your family to turn you into a short-order cook?

9) Have you ever driven to the store for art project materials or school supplies after eight o'clock at night? (The local drugstore often is open late and usually carries an ample supply of everything. That doesn't make it right.) Children need to learn to think ahead.

10) Is your child over ten years old and you still wake him/her up in the morning? Do you make your kid's bed? Clean his or her room? Hmm . . .

11) Do you find yourself missing appointments, whether it be the dentist, doctor, or orthodontist? This could be a sign that you're trying to keep too many other people's schedules in your head. If your child is old enough to have a cell phone, he's old enough to keep track of his own schedule and remind you of where he needs to go/what he needs to do.

12) Are you in a bad mood? Cranky? Stressed? Ask yourself why. Did your child do something? Did he or she "fail"? Are you displeased with your son's or daughter's attitude or grades? Stop. Realize there's a boundary issue *fasho*! (That's how Adelle spells *for sure*.)

13) Do you say you're sorry about things a lot? Are you? Should you be?

14) Do you ever find yourself raising your voice to your kids and the basic contents of the tirade go something like this? "Is anyone going to thank me for breakfast? You know, I don't have to get up and make you a hot breakfast every morning!" The fact is, you don't. And if no one says thank you, then just don't do it. But don't lose your cool. "Your cool" is a very precious thing to hold on to.

15) When you're behind the wheel, do you constantly speed? Are you speeding because it's fun and you don't care how many tickets you get or how high your insurance rates climb? I thought not. Are you speeding because you're late? And are you late because you've tried to pack too much into your day? Is it time to think about cutting back on a few trips? Or perhaps making a child (*gasp*) wait?

◆ ◆ ◆

Are you a major helicopter? Or do you hover just a little? I know, I know . . . it's a stupid little test based on my own personal problems with boundaries. But if any of those silly things did kind of strike a chord in you . . . hey, join the club.

So what if you are in the club? Then what?

I don't know.

See, there. That last sentence proves this book was not written by a man. I admit I don't know what you should do. You're a smart, amazing person. You can figure it all out. Or get some help. That's what I did. I actually learned how to ask for help.

If you lower your guard and admit you're a chopper-mom, so many people in your life will breathe a sigh of relief and say, "I know." Your relentless drive for perfection has not gone unnoticed. Just put it out there. Tell the hubby; tell the kids, the neighbors, the hairdresser, the crossing guard at the school. It's all right. They already know. You're not keeping anything a secret.

My heart is very tender and open toward women who are trying to be all things to all people and losing touch with who they truly are in the process. Let's all push the pause button and abide by the rules of air travel (caution: strange metaphor ahead). Put on YOUR oxygen mask first. THEN help your child with hers.

Our children are not fragile little creatures. Why do we treat them like they're about to get the vapors or faint or collapse from fatigue or complain of being . . . (horror of horrors) thirsty!

I remember one of Helio's football games. It was a coolish fall day. Perfect football weather. Our team kicked off and ran one offensive play in which the quarterback handed the ball to our running back, who traveled about two yards before he was tackled and the play ended. Then the ref called a time-out because he realized they were having some problems with the game clock on the field. Four moms in the stands realized a time-out had been called and they frantically jumped to their feet and pointed and *screamed* in shrill, panicked voices for the coaches to send out the water boys.

"Water! Water! They need water!"

I looked around, dazed—like I was in a dream. Water? Our guys had played exactly 35 SECONDS of football and these moms were worried about their sons' hydration level? I laugh, but then I don't laugh. Know what I mean?

I promise I'm not trying to make fun of anyone. If you've read this far (all the way to the end, God love ya), you know I've mucked up motherhood, career, wife-ness, etc., more than anyone. But that's OK. I'm changing my course. And since I have, my kids are happier and more calm and balanced.

At the Higley house, we don't go to the land of crazy so often. But we don't pretend we've never been there. My family has seen me at my worst, and vice versa. And we still love each other. Maybe we love each other more because, without our company manners and our make-up and fake happy smiles plastered on our faces, we're real . . . blotches, jiggly thighs, and all.

And at the end of the day, I have to admit to everyone that I'm still flawed. I still make mistakes. And I love that I'm loved for me—opinionated, loud, bossy, edgy me. At the same time, I strive every day not to be all those things because I care about the emotional health of my family too much to serve up a healthy diet of whack-o every night.

We're survivors—we Higleys. And it's comforting to know we've been to heck and back several times and we'll always love each other no matter what. This knowledge gives me the courage and the inspiration to change for the better. My friends and family deserve that. And so do I.

And so do you. I saw you today. You were in line (or *online*, if you're from NYC) at the movies today. You were alone, waiting to buy popcorn. I *saw* you. I had you pegged. You were not going to buy popcorn for one. You were not going to buy just one soda. You were there to load up. And sure enough, you did. Three large popcorns, three drinks, candy, pretzels, nachos . . . It was an amazing balancing act. How did I know you were a mom? You had your non-date-night jeans on . . . the comfy ones. You had your sensible flats on . . . big handbag, hair thrown up in a quick ponytail. Some makeup on, but not enough to make your eyes *pop*.

As I watched you gingerly totter back to the seats, my heart swelled with admiration for you—because you're a mom.

If you think no one is appreciating you . . . be assured, I do. I love, adore, and admire you. Take better care of yourself. Give yourself permission to say no. Give yourself permission to fail. Give yourself permission to smile. Give yourself permission to breathe.

As I wrap this whole thing up, I'm prompted to paraphrase the last lines of the movie *Jerry Maguire*. The character of Dicky Fox is sitting behind his desk, summing up his final thoughts about his journey on this planet, and this is my version of what he said:

To be honest, in life, I've failed as much as I've succeeded. But I love my life. I love my family. And I wish you . . . my kind of success.

Ditto, Dicky.

ACKNOWLEDGMENTS

Thank you to everyone whose life story intersected mine in this book. Blessings on my family and friends, and to Jensen's new family, for signing off on the telling of this tale.

I always feel such a deep appreciation for my pastor and friend, Mark Pickerill, for living such an inspiring, spirit-filled, authentic life.

I'm so grateful to Matt Baugher at Thomas Nelson, a very busy man, who was about to board a plane when he called to deliver a very important "yes." Thanks, Matt, for not waiting. Also, a big shout-out to *everyone* at Thomas Nelson, especially my publicity point women, Stephanie and Emily, who stayed up all night to read this book before they met me. Plus, eternal gratitude to my wonderful editor, Adria, whose patience is matched only by her endurance. And I would have been lost without my talented friends, Fran Myers Newman and Lisa Seidman, for proofing my early versions, because you both know I can't.

I will forever be in debt to Aron Gibson for officiating at the "mother of all weddings." You rock!

And thanks most of all to my husband of twenty-five years. Mark, I love you.

ABOUT THE AUTHOR

ena Higley, an Emmy award-winning writer, has been the head writer for both *One Life to Live* and *Days of Our Lives* as well as a playwright in Glendale, CA. She is a graduate of the USC School of Theatre, where she studied acting under the late John Houseman. She currently resides in La Canada-Flintridge, CA, with her husband of twenty-five years, Mark. They have four children and one grandchild.

www.facebook.com/momaholicbook